MEX
TEX

MEX TEX

Traditional Tex-Mex Taste

Matt Martinez

BRIGHT SKY PRESS

BRIGHT SKY PRESS

Box 416
Albany, Texas 76430

10   9   8   7   6   5   4   3   2   1

Library of Congress Cataloging-in-Publication Data

Martinez, Matt, 1945–
   Matt Martinez MexTex : traditional Tex-Mex taste / by Matt G. Martinez Jr.
      p. cm.
   ISBN-13 : 978-1-931721-69-1
   ISBN-10 : 1-931721-69-6 (hardcover : alk. paper)
1. Mexican American cookery. 2. Matt's El Rancho (Restaurant) I. Title.

TX715.2.S69M34 2006
641.5972—dc22

                                                                2006042633

Digital Imaging by Mark Davis, davisstudios.com

Book and cover design by Isabel Lasater Hernandez

Edited by Kristine Krueger

Printed in China through Asia Pacific Offset

DEDICATION

This culinary effort is dedicated to the main source of my cooking inspiration, Janie Martinez.

To my mom, whose hard work and dedication went unnoticed, and at times unappreciated ... that is, except by my dad, Matt Martinez. Dad was a real man in every sense of the word. Charismatic, hospitable, hardworking, he didn't know the meaning of quit or can't. He knew the treasure he had in this woman, whom he loved dearly.

Our family was never neglected, despite the long hours and the heavy kitchen work she took in stride. There is no way to thank her enough or express the love, respect and gratitude this son has.

The Martinez clan—Matt and Estella gather with their children and grandkids on the patio at Matt's Rancho Martinez in Dallas.

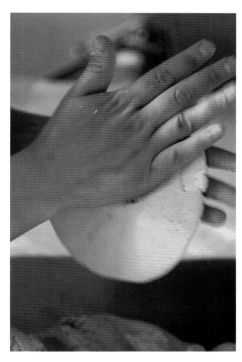

TABLE OF CONTENTS

If you've ever wanted the recipe for Matt's famous Bob Armstrong Dip, you'll find it here ... along with shrimp nachos, quesadillas, margaritas and more.

They're the backbone of Tex-Mex cooking—Matt's special spices and sauces make all the difference.

Matt shows you how to make great fajitas, enchiladas and tacos, along with meats to put in them. Seafood dishes and hearty stews are featured, too.

Beans, rice, pico, veggies, soups and salads ... Matt recommends his favorite accompaniments, including his take on a Caesar.

Start your day off with a kick—make huevos rancheros, burritos or migas for breakfast.

Matt's wife and mom share their specialties for fancy figs, sweet potato custard and Texas pralines. Make your meal complete with a sweet treat.

INTRODUCTION

The inspiration and motivation for *MexTex* came from a world of confusion and misunderstanding, after I saw various recipes on television and the Internet, and heard cooks and chefs express their knowledge or lack of knowledge about Tex-Mex. As a fourth-generation Tex-Mex cook, I felt I had to set the record straight on the simplicity of this cuisine.

MexTex will walk you through the ease of cooking this peasant food that has wowed kings, presidents, statesmen and celebrities from every corner of the world. It's a food that celebrates history, spirit, texture and gastronomical satisfaction.

The term "Tex-Mex fix" was born early and still applies. Once you get into real Tex-Mex, your soul and spirit will cry out for it. *MexTex* will strive to protect its tradition and originality while attempting to perfect what was done right in the first place. Conceived in the 1500s by the Indians and the Spanish, it came to light after the Civil War, with the Chili Queens in San Antonio.

For the uninitiated, the Chili Queens were women who made chili in their homes and transported it in colorful little wagons to San Antonio's Haymarket, Alamo and Military plazas, where they kept it warm over mesquite fires. In fact, during the late 1800s, Military Plaza—the site of what is now city hall—became known as "La Plaza del Chile con Carne" because of these enterprising chili makers.

From those humble beginnings, Tex-Mex has matured into a mighty force in world cuisine.

Appetizers & Drinks

What could be better than a bowl of queso, a basket of chips and an icy margarita? Maybe a shrimp cocktail or guacamole with a tall glass of refreshing sangria. I've shared some of the restaurant's most-requested appetizers … including, of course, my "Bob dip" and my "smoked Bob"— which features smoked brisket instead of taco meat. They'll make any hour happy hour!

TRADITIONAL GUACAMOLE

About two dozen varieties of avocados are grown in the U.S. The ones with black skin and a pebbly texture, like the California Hass, are my favorite.

Select your avocados by pressing on the skin. If it gives a little but does not leave a dent, it is okay for slicing or making guacamole. If it leaves a small dent, it is okay for guacamole but too ripe for slicing. A large dent indicates it is overripe.

Hard avocados ripen at room temperature in three to four days. When they're ripe, keep avocados in the refrigerator and use within two to three days.

Cut the avocado in half. Discard the pit and scoop out the avocado flesh into a bowl; discard the skin. Mash the juice into the avocado and continue mashing until guacamole reaches desired texture. For the best texture, leave it chunky. Adjust salt to taste.

Suggested Side Garnishes: Finely chopped sweet white onion, fresh cilantro or jalapeño ... crushed and finely chopped garlic ... finely chopped seeded tomato ... Pico de Gallo or Virgin Pico (recipes on pages 152 and 153).

1 avocado

1 teaspoon freshly squeezed lime *or* lemon juice

Salt to taste

MAKES 2 SERVINGS

My father, Matt Martinez Sr., opened Matt's El Rancho in Austin in 1952.

CHILE CON QUESO

1½ cups green chiles (canned *or* fresh, peeled and finely diced)

½ cup diced fresh tomato

½ cup diced onion

½ cup diced celery

2 teaspoons Tex-Mex Spice (recipe on page 41)

1 cup chicken broth

1 pound American cheese, cubed

In a saucepan, combine all ingredients except cheese. Bring to a light simmer and gently cook for about 5 minutes. Turn heat down and add the cheese. Simmer until cheese is melted. Add water if it's too thick or more cheese if it's too thin.

Variations: If you don't have green chiles, you can substitute green bell peppers.

For extra-spicy queso, reduce green chiles to 1 cup and add ¹/₂ cup of diced fresh serranos or jalapeños.

MAKES 3 CUPS

ROASTING YOUR OWN PEPPERS FOR CHILE CON QUESO

Use Anaheim or poblano chiles. Preheat oven to 500°. Rub chiles with olive oil. Place on a baking sheet. Anaheim chiles will take about 14 minutes, while poblanos will take a full 15 minutes. It is important to turn the peppers over once halfway through the roasting time.

When they're done, place the peppers in an ice bath to stop the cooking process. Open the pepper, remove the seeds and rinse in the ice bath. Peel off as much skin as possible. Now they are ready for frying, dicing or chopping. They also freeze well in ziplock bags.

BOB ARMSTRONG DIP

Our most famous appetizer. Here's the story behind how this dip got its name: Years ago, I was in the kitchen working "90 to nuthin" in charge of salads and appetizers. Since I was the owner's teenage son, the other employees liked to watch me run out of stuff or get confused. I really had to stay on my toes, which meant being prepared for anything.

One day, Bob Armstrong, a longtime politician who had been Land Commissioner of Texas, walked into the kitchen. "Little Matt," he said, "gimme something different for an appetizer ... something not on the menu."

I replied, "Go sit down, it's on its way." I grabbed whatever jumped into my hands. I threw some taco meat in the bottom of a bowl, and I threw in guacamole and sour cream. Then I made some chile con queso, poured it over the top and put it all in the oven.

The waitress later told me when she took it out to him, Mr. Armstrong muttered, "That ain't nothing but a bowl of queso." Then he stuck his spoon in there and saw guacamole, sour cream and some beef. He hushed up for a while and started eating. Then his eyes got as big as saucers.

I had the next day off, so I went fishing. Customers kept coming into El Rancho and ordering "that Bob Armstrong dip that's not on the menu," but nobody at the restaurant had any idea what the clamor was all about. I got in trouble, and I wasn't even there.

What we didn't realize was Mr. Armstrong had gone back to the State Capitol after lunch that day and told everybody about this amazing appetizer he'd had. When I went to work the following day, the orders kept coming in. I barely remembered the recipe because I'd simply been throwing whatever was nearby into the bowl.

4 recipes of Traditional Guacamole (page 19)
1 recipe of 20-Minute Taco Meat (page 95)
1 recipe of Chile con Queso (page 20)

Warm a 9-inch x 13-inch or 7-inch x 11-inch pan. Spread guacamole into the pan, then add a layer of hot taco meat. Top with hot chile con queso. Serve with chips, chalupa shells or tortillas of your choice. Garnish with pico, sour cream or your favorite hot sauce.

MAKES 16 TO 20 SERVINGS

★ 23

MATT'S FAMOUS SMOKED BOB

You can also serve this as a main dish for 4 to 6 people.

1 recipe Chile con Queso (page 20)
4 cups shredded smoked brisket
1 recipe Traditional Guacamole (page 19)
1 cup (8 ounces) sour cream
Green onions and jalapeños for garnish
12 to 16 flour tortillas

Prepare the queso and pour some on a warm plate. Put the shredded brisket over the queso in the middle of the plate. Lop the guacamole and sour cream on the queso just to the side of the brisket. Garnish with green onion and jalapeño.

Serve with tortillas and mix tastes to your heart's desire. Use the tortillas to sop up the queso, or fill them with brisket, queso, sour cream and guacamole.

MAKES 6 TO 8 SERVINGS

STUFFED JALAPEÑOS

Slit open one side of each jalapeño and discard all the seeds and membranes. Rinse jalapeños in cold water and pat dry. Stuff with cheese. Roll the peppers in flour, dunk them in the buttermilk, then roll in the cracker meal. Place in the freezer for about 2 to 3 hours, until they are completely frozen.

Using enough oil to give you about an inch in depth, fry the peppers to a golden brown at 350°. Hold in a warm oven for 10 to 15 minutes before serving.

MAKES 4 TO 6 SERVINGS

12 whole pickled jalapeños
2 cups (8 ounces) shredded
   Monterey Jack *or* American cheese
1 cup flour
2 cups buttermilk
2 cups cracker meal *or* seasoned
   bread crumbs
Oil of your choice for deep frying

CHORIZO BEAN DIP

Layer the beans and chorizo in a 9-inch x 13-inch casserole dish. Bake at 350° for 10 minutes. Pour warm queso over the top. Serve with chips, chalupa shells or tortillas of your choice.

MAKES 8 TO 10 SERVINGS

4 cups refried beans
4 cups cooked chorizo
3 cups chile con queso

A MEXTEX FEATURE

PERFECT QUESADILLAS

In a skillet over medium heat, first warm the tortillas until barely brown; remove and stack. If using *only* meat, beans or veggies, place the filling on one side of each tortilla. If using *both* meat and beans, first mix them together in a bowl, then spread over one side of tortillas. (I like to use a #16 ice cream scoop to distribute the filling. It holds the perfect amount per tortilla.) Top with cheese. Fold tortilla over like a taco.

Baste the top side with butter. Put the butter/cheese side down in skillet. On medium-high, cook to a golden brown. Baste the top side; flip and cook until the other side is golden brown. Place on a platter in a warm oven until ready to serve. Serve with hot sauce, sour cream, guacamole and pico.

*PREFERRED FILLINGS

Taco meat
Taco meat and pinto beans
Black beans
Pinto beans
Veggies
Suggested raw veggies—chopped onion or bell pepper, minced broccoli or cauliflower, baby spinach (no more than 12 leaves), chopped or thinly sliced zucchini or squash.

Flour tortillas (8-inch size)
½ cup filling of choice per tortilla*
2 ounces shredded American,
   Monterey Jack *or* cheddar cheese
   per tortilla
Butter for basting

PERFECT QUESADILLAS

FRESHWATER CEVICHE

You can use any type of freshwater bass or crappie for this appetizer.

2½ to 3 pounds freshwater whitefish
1 medium tomato, halved and thinly sliced
1 onion, very coarsely chopped
1 cup virgin olive oil
½ cup red wine vinegar
½ cup fresh lemon juice
½ cup chopped fresh cilantro (loosely packed)
2 tablespoons brown sugar
1 heaping tablespoon crushed garlic
2 teaspoons salt
1 teaspoon black pepper
4 limes, cut into wedges
2 lemons, cut into wedges

Cut the fish into ¼-inch strips. In a large bowl, mix all the other ingredients except limes and lemons. Pour the mixture into an airtight plastic storage bag; add fish strips and blend thoroughly. Press the air from the bag and seal. Pack the bag in ice for a minimum of 1 hour but no more than 2, or refrigerate for 2 to 3 hours. Serve ceviche cold with limes and lemons to squeeze over. Garnish with diced avocado, sliced jalapeños and red pepper strips if desired.

MAKES 8 TO 10 SERVINGS

LITTLE MATT'S SHRIMP COCKTAIL

3 pounds cooked small shrimp, shelled and deveined

Cocktail Sauce:

1 bottle (14 ounces) ketchup

1 can (11½ ounces) V8 juice

Juice of 2 lemons

½ cup Sprite *or* 7UP

½ cup diced fresh tomato

¼ cup chopped onion

¼ cup chopped jalapeños

2 teaspoons salt

1 teaspoon Worcestershire sauce

1 teaspoon black pepper

¼ cup thinly sliced celery, *divided*

Garnish:

2 avocados, peeled and thinly sliced

1 bunch cilantro, finely chopped

2 lemons, cut into wedges

My son created this cocktail sauce, which I always use for shrimp cocktail. I like to make the sauce a day in advance so it can chill overnight.

Chill the shrimp until ready to serve. Combine all of the sauce ingredients except for half of the celery; mix well. (I like to use a pitcher for mixing.) Cover with lid or plastic wrap and refrigerate.

To serve, sprinkle the remaining celery into eight tall glasses (parfait glasses work well). Fill each glass evenly with shrimp. Stir cocktail sauce well and pour equal amounts over shrimp. Place avocado slices on top and garnish with cilantro. Serve lemon wedges and crispy crackers on the side. Provide a small bowl of Bad Boy Hot Sauce (page 49) for those who like it hotter.

MAKES 8 SERVINGS

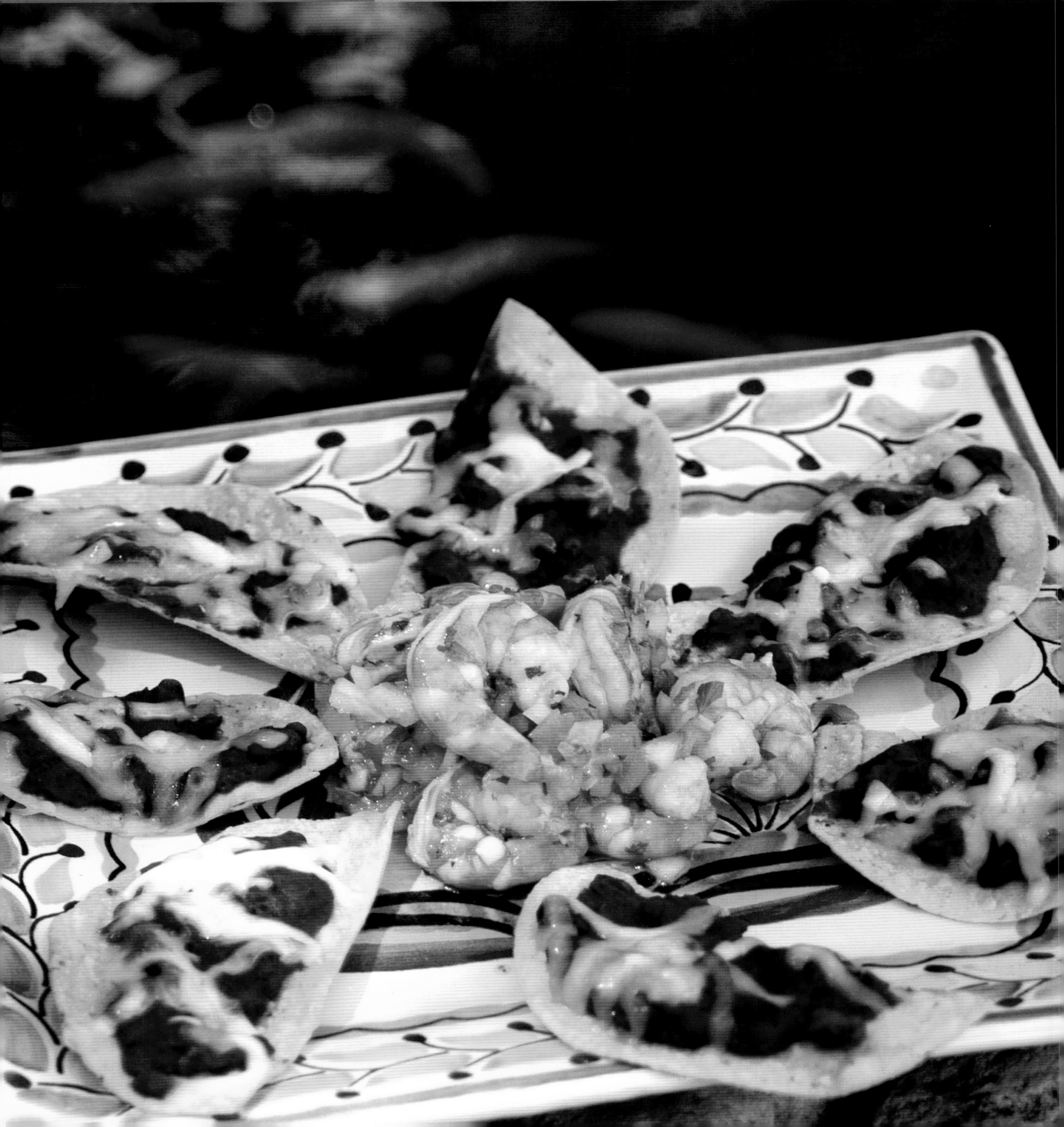

TEXAS SHRIMP NACHOS

For these nachos, I prefer sautéing the shrimp, but any method will work.

Break chalupa shells in half. Spread beans on each half with a spoon or knife. Top with shrimp and cheese. Place on a baking sheet. Bake for 4 to 4½ minutes at 450°, or broil for 2 minutes on the middle rack. Check your broiler to prevent burning. A little charring on the cheese is really good. Garnish with pico, sour cream and hot sauce of your choice.

4 chalupa shells
1 cup mashed pinto *or* black beans
¼ pound cooked shrimp, thinly sliced
1 cup (4 ounces) shredded American, Monterey Jack *or* cheddar cheese

MAKES 4 SERVINGS

Estella and I toast on our wedding day, March 1, 1969.

A MEXTEX FEATURE

SUMMER SANGRIA

In a pitcher, combine the water, lime juice and sugar. Fill a glass with ice. Fill up three-quarters of the glass with the juice mixture. Fill the remaining quarter with red wine. (I like to use a dry red table wine.) Garnish with an orange ring and maraschino cherry.

1 quart water
1 cup fresh lime juice
1 cup sugar
Red wine of your choice

MAKES 4 TO 6 SERVINGS

SUMMER SANGRIA

BORDER BLOODY MARY

1 rib celery with leaves, coarsely chopped
1 whole chipotle pepper in adobo sauce*
1 can (46 ounces) tomato juice, chilled, *divided*
1 clove garlic, thinly sliced
½ cup orange juice, chilled
½ cup fresh lemon juice
2 tablespoons Worcestershire sauce
2 tablespoons horseradish
1 teaspoon black pepper
1 teaspoon salt

Add celery, chipotle pepper, 2 cups tomato juice and garlic to a blender; cover and puree. Pour into a large pitcher; add the remaining tomato juice and all other ingredients. Stir well. Adjust salt and pepper to taste. Refrigerate until chilled.

To serve, salt half of the rim of a 6-ounce glass. Add 1 ounce of chilled tequila to 4 ounces chilled Bloody Mary mixture; stir. Serve with a lime wedge and garnish with finely chopped cilantro. I prefer to use a white tequila (Sauza silver is my favorite).

*Chipotle pepper in adobo sauce (which comes in a 7-ounce can) is my first choice because of the smoky flavor. To add a little heat to this Bloody Mary, other options are 1 tablespoon Bad Boy Hot Sauce (Dry Chile Variation—adjust quantity to suit desired heat—recipe on page 49) ... or one pickled jalapeño pepper (plus jalapeño juice if more heat is desired).

MAKES 8 TO 10 SERVINGS

MATT'S BASIC MARGARITA

¼ cup sugar
½ cup fresh lime juice, chilled
1½ cups cold water
¼ cup Grand Marnier

In a pitcher, combine all of the ingredients. Use 1 part tequila to 4 parts margarita mixture. Serve over ice with a wedge of lime.

Variation: Instead of Grand Marnier, use the same quantity of Cointreau or De Kuyper triple sec.

Poor Boy Margarita: Double the sugar and eliminate the Grand Marnier.

MAKES 4 SERVINGS

PERRO SALADO ("SALTY DOG")

1½ ounces tequila
4 ounces freshly squeezed grapefruit juice

Salt the rim of an 8-ounce glass. Fill with ice. Add tequila and grapefruit juice; stir and enjoy. Garnish with lime wedge. You can use more or less tequila, depending on your preference (I prefer Sauza silver).

MAKES 1 SERVING

Spices & Sauces

Simplicity rules when it comes to seasoning Tex-Mex food. I think you'll be amazed at the spectacular results from the simple combination of cumin or cornmeal, garlic, salt and pepper. Plus, I'll show you how to make your own hot sauces—as mild or hot as you like—and enchilada sauces. With my recipes, you'll serve Tex-Mex with confidence.

Estella's parents, Gustavo Benavidez and Nicanora Ruiz Benavidez.

In early Texas, the best ingredients might have been a jackrabbit or a fat armadillo, some wild onions, peppers or tender cactus leaves growing along the creeks and rivers. Cooking with a handicap brought out the best in early Texas chefs. It created a cuisine that reflects the ingenuity and resourcefulness these campfire wizards developed.

Making something out of nothing came into focus when I watched and cooked with some of these seasoned cooks like my mother, grandmother and mother-in-law. These ladies mastered the art of making do.

MexTex will not have an abundance of exotic spices, meats and vegetables, but it hopes to capture the efforts of those who blazed the trail to Tex-Mex. The infusions, reductions and presentation you might hear other chefs talk about will not have a big part in this book.

Tex-Mex got its infusion 500 years ago from the Spanish, the Indians, and others who migrated from all over the country and the far corners of the world. People traveling to Texas or just passing through faced the possibility of running into drought, famine, disease, wild Indians, bandits or one of Santa Anna's armies. Even such looming threats couldn't chase these hardy souls away from their dreams.

Tex-Mex has settled in its evolution and is slowing because we are content with our efforts. Except for the instruments and tools we use, there have been very few changes in the last 100 years. In addition, the availability of fresh and ground spices, chiles, veggies, meats and seafood has added convenience.

The sauces that give variety and uniqueness are the lifeblood of this Texas blessing. Red chile, ranchero, green sauce and hot sauce are the oldies, with the "Johnny-come-lately" cream and queso sauces bringing up the rear.

TEX-MEX SPICE

When we salt and pepper different foods, it doesn't make them taste the same. I use the same principle with these seasonings, except that I have added two more ingredients—garlic and cumin.

Proteins, carbohydrates and oils change the character of a spice. So you can cook chili, taco meat, rice, sauces and so on, and your family, friends or customers will never know it's the same seasoning. This spice will have a fantastic blend that is light in salt. Carefully adjust the salt if needed.

This spice mix responds best when it is slightly browned during the cooking process. We will use this mix for most of our dishes. It keeps well in an airtight container or ziplock bag.

3 tablespoons plus 2 teaspoons ground cumin

3 tablespoons granulated garlic

2 tablespoons salt

1 tablespoon coarsely ground black pepper

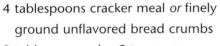

TEXAS SPRINKLE

Salt, pepper, garlic and cornmeal. This spice mix will bring into focus the fact that simplicity rules. It is user-friendly and forgiving. I'll give you amounts to use at first, but you will be sprinkling it freely with confidence very soon.

4 tablespoons cracker meal *or* finely ground unflavored bread crumbs

3 tablespoons plus 2 teaspoons granulated garlic

3 tablespoons salt

2 tablespoons coarsely ground black pepper

When combined with Black Magic, this spice will take you into a new dimension and will hopefully bring ease, confidence and consistency to your cooking.

Rule of thumb for meat, chicken and seafood: Use 1 teaspoon per 4 ounces. For veggies: Use 1 teaspoon per 2 cups.

BLACK MAGIC FINISHING SAUCE

Black Magic came about from an adventure in the kitchen of a Chinese restaurant in Austin belonging to a friend of my father.

I originally had an aversion to marinating because of the inconsistency in a restaurant environment, and the fact that my mother never marinated foods. But through a complex trial-and-error process came this very simple finishing sauce rich in flavor, aroma and color. Black Magic doesn't reveal its ingredients in the finished product—it only enhances the finished product.

The name came from our cooks—after they saw and tasted what the sauce would do to either flame-grilled or flat-grilled foods. You will also see that it is truly magic.

Use red wine vinegar of your choice, except balsamic. Cabernet Sauvignon is my first choice in red wines, but others will work. Leave port wines for other uses.

This sauce actually stimulates food. The physical reaction it has on food is as important as the flavor it lends. Rule of thumb: Use 1 teaspoon per 4 ounces of veggies, meats, chicken or seafood.

Black Magic should be added at the end of the cooking process. When the product is cooked the way you want it, add the sauce, flip and coat evenly. Let the sauce meet the heat to do its work. Black Magic will react to a hot skillet or open flame. When cooking indoors, it may cause a little smoke, so turn your overhead vent on high.

This sauce keeps very well in an airtight container, but it's so good, it will get used up quickly!

1 bottle (10 ounces) Kikkoman light soy sauce
⅓ cup red wine vinegar
⅓ cup red wine

HOMEMADE CHILE POWDER

You can use this spice in my enchilada sauce recipes.

1 bag (5 ounces) chile ancho peppers
3 tablespoons paprika
1 teaspoon olive oil

Rinse ancho peppers and dry thoroughly. It is best to wash peppers a day before usage or even blow-dry them. Anchos need to be totally dry.

Clip stems with scissors; open peppers and shake out seeds. Spread open peppers and flatten. Place on a paper plate (do not use Styrofoam or plastic). Microwave on high for 1 minute. Cool for 5 minutes and then repeat the process.

Feel peppers after the third time. Depending on the freshness of the peppers, the process may take three to five zaps in the microwave. Because of the oil in the peppers, they will not be crisp when warm. Let cool for 5 minutes before checking the crispness.

When crisp, break up the peppers, using your hands, and put in a food processor. Grind until they look like fine ground coffee. When ground, add paprika and olive oil. Grind one more time, for approximately 5 seconds, to mix.

Note: To make sure you don't burn the chiles in the microwave, test one first. You may need to reduce the heating time depending on the wattage of your microwave. Also, it is a good idea to wear plastic gloves when working with peppers.

You can vary this method, if you want to suffer the failures I did. The old method is to open and seed the anchos, bake at 200° for 12 hours, then break up and grind.

CHILI AND CHILE

There is *chili* powder and there is *chile* powder. Chili powder is a combination of ground chiles, cumin, oregano, garlic, salt and sometimes powdered onion. Pick your pleasure from a variety of brands and mixes. Chile powder is a combination of certain ground and powdered chiles.

Confused? Well, as a youngster, so was I. I decided to start making my own chili powder and chile powder, and then I knew exactly what I had to work with. In a pinch, I'd go with Gebhardt for a store-bought chile, but there are many to choose from.

I don't mix an assortment of chiles and try to get a magic blend, because there are too many variables in the peppers. I stick with chile ancho, which is the most consistent packaged chile. There are two things to check when buying chile ancho—that they're bright red and pliable. Go ahead and bend and twist them in the package. If brittle, they're not fresh. If the two criteria are met, we can go to work making something good to eat.

Trying to stay out of trouble in 1953.

"My daddy was always working, so my uncle took me fishing. My grandmother was one of my main inspirations when it came to cooking. She always sent me out with a little waxed paper packet of spices—salt, pepper and garlic powder—when I went hunting. I'd kill a bird, wipe it off with my T-shirt and roast it in a fire. We ate a lot of birds back then."

CHILE DE HOYA

This is my home-style hot sauce.

In a small pot, put jalapeños down first. Add the remaining ingredients. Gently simmer for 30 to 45 minutes (until peppers are soft). Let cool.

Remove peppers. Put the other ingredients in a blender or food processor; add half of the peppers. Coarsely chop in processor. Taste for heat and salt. Blend in additional peppers gradually to reach your desired level of heat.

Variations: You can substitute a 14$^1/_2$-ounce can of whole tomatoes for the fresh tomatoes if desired. For cilantro lovers, add $^1/_4$ cup loosely packed cilantro at the blending step.

To make it real home-style, in lieu of the blender or food processor, mash the mixture in the cooking pot with a potato masher or spoon.

MAKES ABOUT 1 QUART

4 to 6 fresh jalapeños
1 pound red tomatoes (Roma or vine-ripened are best)
1 cup chopped onion
½ cup water
2 tablespoons olive oil
1 tablespoon vinegar
2 teaspoons chopped garlic
1 teaspoon Tex-Mex Spice (recipe on page 41)
1 teaspoon salt

QUICK HOT SAUCE

Make hot sauce in 3 minutes!

Blend or process all ingredients. The ice cubes slice well—a half cube (or 1 tablespoon) with one 14$^1/_2$-ounce can of tomatoes will be mild. One cube (or 2 tablespoons) will be hot, and so on.

Variations: For more flavor, you can add 1 to 2 tablespoons minced white onion or 1 to 2 tablespoons chopped cilantro.

For a hot sauce like Pace, sauté $^1/_4$ cup chopped onion with 1 teaspoon olive oil. When limp, blend with tomatoes.

MAKES 2 CUPS

1 can of your favorite canned whole tomatoes
Bad Boy Hot Sauce ice cubes (recipe on page 49)
Salt to taste

★ 47

BAD BOY HOT SAUCE ("BAD BASTARD")

There are two variations of this sauce, made with either fresh or dry chiles. Both sauces freeze very well in ice cube trays. Most trays have 16 slots and hold 2 tablespoons of sauce per slot. When frozen, I pop them out and place in ziplock bags. Keep in the freezer and use to spice up stews, soups or Bloody Marys or to make hot sauce.

Fresh Chile Variation:

1 cup coarsely chopped onion

3 tablespoons olive oil

1 tablespoon flour

1½ cups water

1 tablespoon salt

1 ounce garlic (3 tablespoons coarsely chopped)

8 ounces fresh serrano chiles *or* jalapeños

2 tablespoons red wine vinegar

In a saucepan, sauté onion in oil on medium heat until translucent. Add flour. Sauté 2 to 3 more minutes. Add water, salt, garlic and fresh chiles. Cook on low heat for 25 to 30 minutes. Let cool.

Add vinegar. Puree in a food processor or blender. Store in an airtight container. This stuff is very hot ... a little goes a long way!

Dry Chile Variation:

1 cup coarsely chopped onion

3 tablespoons olive oil

1 tablespoon flour

2 cups water

1 tablespoon salt

1 ounce garlic (3 tablespoons coarsely chopped)

1 ounce dry chiles*

2 tablespoons red wine vinegar

In a saucepan, sauté onion in oil on medium heat until translucent. Add flour. Sauté 2 to 3 more minutes. Add water, salt, garlic and dry chiles. Cook on low heat for 1 hour, stirring once or twice. Make sure it does not go dry. Let cool.

Add vinegar. Puree in a food processor or blender. Strain and squeeze with a spoon to remove all liquid. Discard seeds and pepper skin. Add water to make 2 cups. It's ready to use or freeze. Store in an airtight container.

*Use pequin, arbol, cayenne, Japanese, jalapeño or chipotle for an outdoor smoky flavor. It is okay to mix different kinds of peppers to equal 1 ounce.

MAKES 2 CUPS

TOMATILLO HOT SAUCE

4 to 6 fresh jalapeños

1 pound green Mexican tomatillos with husks (remove husks before using)

1 cup chopped onion

3 chicken bouillon cubes

½ cup water

2 tablespoons olive oil

1 tablespoon vinegar

2 teaspoons chopped garlic

¼ cup fresh cilantro (loosely packed)

In a small pot, put jalapeños down first. Add the tomatillos, onion, bouillon cubes, water, oil, vinegar and garlic. Gently simmer for 30 to 45 minutes (until peppers are soft). Let cool.

Remove peppers. Put the other ingredients in a blender or food processor; add cilantro and half of the peppers. Coarsely chop in processor. Taste for heat. Blend in additional peppers gradually to reach your desired level of heat.

MAKES ABOUT 1 QUART

SOUR CREAM SAUCE FOR ENCHILADAS

In a heavy skillet on low to medium heat, sauté onion in butter and flour until translucent. Add celery and cook 1 more minute. Turn heat off and transfer mixture to a double boiler. Stir in milk, water and bouillon. Simmer for 4 to 5 minutes. Mix in sour cream. When sauce is slightly warm, it is ready to serve.

MAKES ABOUT 1 QUART

1 cup finely diced onion
½ cup butter
½ cup flour
1 cup finely diced celery
1 cup whole milk
1 cup water
3 chicken bouillon cubes *or* 3 teaspoons chicken bouillon granules
2 pints sour cream

RANCHERO SAUCE

This is the sauce used for catfish, steak or chicken tampiqueno, chiles rellenos, huevos rancheros, tostada compuestas and enchiladas. Instead of bell pepper, try using green chiles, such as ancho or Anaheim chiles. For a more piquant version, see the variation below.

3 tablespoons vegetable oil (canola, peanut, etc.)

1 cup chopped white *or* yellow onion

½ cup chopped celery

½ cup chopped bell pepper

2 tablespoons Tex-Mex Spice (recipe on page 41)

3 tablespoons all-purpose flour

2 cups chicken broth

1 can (8 ounces) tomato sauce

1 can (14½ ounces) whole tomatoes

Water, if needed

Heat oil over medium heat in a 1-quart saucepan or 10-inch cast-iron skillet. Add onion, celery and bell pepper. Turn down heat and cook just until onion is translucent. Do not allow vegetables to brown. Add Tex-Mex Spice and flour, mixing well. Simmer until flour begins to color, about 3 to 4 minutes, watching carefully to prevent burning.

Add the chicken broth, tomato sauce and whole tomatoes. With a flat spatula, scrape bottom of pan and break up tomatoes into sauce. Turn heat to low and let sauce simmer gently for 25 to 30 minutes. Add water, if necessary, to make 1 quart.

Variation: Add three whole jalapeños to the sauce when mixing in the tomatoes. Remove jalapeños and set aside. After gently cooking for 25 to 30 minutes, break up one jalapeños in a small bowl and stir back into the sauce. Taste. If additional heat is desired, continue adding jalapeños to taste.

For Vegetarian Sauce: Replace the 2 cups of chicken broth with water.

MAKES 1 QUART

EASY CHILI CON CARNE

This is my mother's original recipe. It makes a nice enchilada sauce and is great for making chili dogs. Leftovers are good with scrambled eggs.

2 pounds coarse ground chuck

1 teaspoon vegetable oil

1 cup chopped fresh tomatoes

½ cup chopped onion

½ cup chopped bell pepper

3 cloves garlic, mashed into paste

4 tablespoons chili powder

1 tablespoon paprika

1½ teaspoons salt

½ teaspoon ground cumin

Pinch of oregano

4 cups water

2 tablespoons masa harina, mixed
    with sufficient water to make paste

Brown beef in a large saucepan, using the oil to prevent scorching. Cook over medium heat until nicely browned, stirring frequently. Add remaining ingredients except for water and masa; mix thoroughly. Continue to cook over low heat, uncovered, for about 10 minutes, stirring frequently so meat doesn't stick to the bottom.

Stir in the water. Cover and continue to cook over low heat for about 45 minutes or until meat is nice and tender. Adjust seasoning as necessary. When meat is tender, add masa paste and mix well. Cook on low heat, uncovered, for 20 more minutes.

Serve in individual bowls topped with shredded cheese and chopped onions, with crackers or bread on the side. It's also good with beans (not refried) on the side.

Variation: You can use canned stewed tomatoes in place of the fresh tomatoes.

MAKES 4 TO 6 SERVINGS

Before becoming serious about
restaurants, my father was a boxer.

★ 55

BEEF ENCHILADA SAUCE

1 pound ground beef

½ cup chopped onion

½ cup chopped bell pepper

3 tablespoons plus 1 teaspoon
Tex-Mex Spice (recipe on page 41)

2 tablespoons chili powder

1 teaspoon paprika

2 cups water

1 can (14½ ounces) whole tomatoes,
diced *or* crushed

Combine all ingredients except for water and tomatoes. Place in a cold skillet or sauté pan. On medium heat, cook for 6 to 8 minutes (until onion is translucent). Add water and tomatoes. Simmer gently for 1 hour; stir and scrape the pan occasionally to make sure the sauce doesn't stick.

MAKES ABOUT 1 QUART

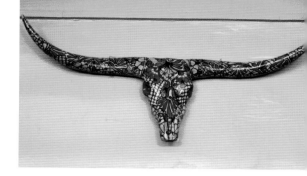

TEXAS ORIGINAL ENCHILADA SAUCE

Add flour and lard to a heavy skillet. Brown for 2 to 3 minutes. Add Tex-Mex Spice, stirring with a flat spatula for 1 to 2 minutes on low heat. Be careful not to let it burn. Add chili powder; mix well for 1 minute.

Add chicken broth, water and tomato sauce. Stir and scrape with spatula. Add peanut butter and bring to a light simmer. Let sauce simmer on low heat, stirring and scraping bottom of pan, for 5 to 10 minutes. Let thicken slightly.

Taste. If you like it a little hotter, add a Bad Boy ice cube or some refrigerated Bad Boy Hot Sauce (recipe on page 49). The dry chile recipe is a little better in this one. Remember, a little goes a long way!

MAKES 1 QUART

8 tablespoons flour

8 tablespoons lard *or* duck, chicken *or* pork drippings

3 tablespoons Tex-Mex Spice (recipe on page 41)

2 tablespoons chili powder

3 cups low-sodium chicken broth

½ cup water

1 can (8 ounces) tomato sauce

1 tablespoon creamy peanut butter

Celebrating with my parents, Janie and Matt Martinez Sr., and sisters (back row from left) Gloria, Cathy and Cecilia.

2006 TEXAS ENCHILADA SAUCE

In a heavy skillet or pan, sauté Tex-Mex Spice in oil, gently stirring with a flat spatula until you can smell the spices, approximately 2 minutes. Add chili powder and stir for 1 minute. Add chicken broth, tomato sauce and peanut butter, then bring to a simmer.

Mix cornstarch and water in a small bowl until cornstarch is totally dissolved and smooth. While sauce is simmering, drizzle in cornstarch mixture, stirring with spatula for 1 minute. Cook for 5 to 10 minutes on low heat. Stir occasionally to prevent sticking.

Taste. If you want it a little hotter, mix in a Bad Boy ice cube or refrigerated sauce (recipe on page 49). Remember, a little goes a long way! A serving of this sauce has only 1 tablespoon of fat.

MAKES 1 QUART

3 tablespoons Tex-Mex Spice (recipe on page 41)

1 tablespoon olive oil

2 tablespoons chili powder

3 cups low-sodium chicken broth

1 can (8 ounces) tomato sauce

1 tablespoon creamy peanut butter

4 tablespoons cornstarch

½ cup water

2006 TEXAS ENCHILADA SAUCE

GREEN SIMPLICITY TOMATILLO SAUCE

You can use this sauce as a base for the Creamy Enchilada Sauce (below) and the Cold Tomatillo Cream Soup on page 132.

2 cups chopped onions
3 tablespoons olive oil
2 teaspoons fresh garlic
3 tablespoons flour
1 teaspoon salt
1 teaspoon sugar
2 cups chicken broth
1 pound tomatillos, husks removed
  and quartered
½ cup fresh cilantro (loosely packed)
4 fresh jalapeños

In a heavy stockpot, sauté onions in oil on low heat until they're translucent. Add garlic, flour, salt and sugar. Stir and cook for 2 to 3 minutes, being careful not to burn onions. Add chicken broth; stir. Add tomatillos, cilantro and whole jalapeños. Gently stir and simmer for 30 to 45 minutes.

When jalapeños are soft, it is ready. Remove three jalapeños. Crush sauce with a potato masher, or cool and gently blend or process in a blender. Taste for salt and spice. If you want it hotter, crush one jalapeño and add back in. Add one at a time for desired heat. Add water to make 1 quart.

MAKES 1 QUART

CREAMY ENCHILADA SAUCE

1 recipe Green Simplicity Tomatillo
  Sauce (recipe above)
1 cup (8 ounces) sour cream

To make smooth and creamy enchilada sauce, strain Tomatillo Sauce in a colander, mashing the veggies to get as much juice as possible. Cool slightly; discard pulp. Add sour cream and blend thoroughly. It's ready for enchiladas.

MAKES ABOUT 1 QUART

CILANTRO CREAM SAUCE

This sauce is a good option to use in dishes that call for hollandaise sauce.

2 tablespoons minced fresh onion

2 tablespoons butter

2 tablespoons flour

2 tablespoons minced fresh tomato

2 tablespoons minced fresh jalapeños
  or serranos

2 tablespoons minced celery

¼ cup water

2 tablespoons sour cream

2 cups half-and-half cream

2 tablespoons finely chopped fresh
  cilantro (loosely packed)

In a heavy skillet on low to medium heat, sauté onion in butter until translucent. Add flour and sauté 1 to 2 minutes until slightly brown. Be careful not to burn. Add tomato, peppers, celery and water. Simmer until pan is almost dry. Let cool.

Transfer mixture to a double boiler. Stir in sour cream. Under low heat, stir in half-and-half; heat through but be careful not to let it boil. When sauce is warm, sprinkle in cilantro and serve.

MAKES 1 QUART

CILANTRO VINAIGRETTE

1 cup olive oil
½ cup red wine vinegar
½ cup fresh cilantro (loosely packed)
1 tablespoon crushed and chopped garlic
2 teaspoons salt
1 teaspoon black pepper

Place all ingredients in a blender; cover and blend for 30 seconds. Transfer to an airtight container and refrigerate until chilled. Shake or stir vigorously before using.

MAKES 1½ CUPS

Longtime employees of Matt's Rancho Martinez in Dallas. Back row (left to right): Martin Zisman, Alejandro Garcia, Apolinar Garcia, Steve Brewer and Vicki La Grange. Front row: Matias Macias and Jesus Cabrera.

Matt's Mains

Now you are ready to put my spices and sauces to work making fantastic enchiladas, chalupas, fajitas and lots more. With a variety of meats, seafood, cheeses and tortillas, you'll have endless options to mix and match. Using basic, readily available ingredients indigenous to America, Tex-Mex is "good time food" that's also good for you.

My parents, Matt Martinez Sr. and Janie Gaitan Martinez, on their wedding day, July 27, 1944.

"My father was a local hero. Back when the dining halls at UT weren't open on Sundays, some of the students who were regular customers would come in. They wouldn't have any money to pay until Monday or even Friday, but my father would feed them anyway."

When I was about halfway through the third grade, I realized I'd reached my goals in life. I could read comic books and the funny papers ... I could forge my parents' signatures pretty well ... and I could write a sad excuse when I didn't go to school.

I used to get up in the morning and grab my BB gun from under the front porch. I'd leave my shoes there and head off to the creek. You see, I wanted to be a professional bird hunter. But when the wily birds weren't cooperating, I got really hungry. So I'd take a break every once in a while and go to school with a note saying I'd been sick.

My dad would give me 25 cents for lunch, but I'd go through the line barefoot and act like I didn't have any money. Feeling sorry for me, the teachers would buy my lunch. So I'd have 25 cents for BBs. At a nickel a pack, and 100 BBs to a pack, I had 500 BBs. Can you believe that?

Things were really going good until the end of school, when my teachers sent a letter home saying I had failed third grade 'cause I had been sick too much that year. Mama went marching up to that school and told them her son hadn't missed a day of school—he's never sick. Then they showed her the notes.

Oh, I guess you could call it a good beatin' I got all the way home. And it was private school for me for the rest of my life.

It was an awful thing to happen to a professional bird hunter like me, but you know, it's one of those professions that don't last forever. I did eat a lot of birds, though. Not enough to get fat, but it was a good experience, a really good experience. It sharpened my cooking skills.

CARNE GUISADA

This flavorful stew-like dish can be made with beef or chicken (see Pollo Guisada on page 68). The meat gets nice and tender while it cooks slowly on the stove.

In a 4-quart heavy skillet or pot, add oil and bring to medium heat. When oil is hot, add meat and sauté for 10 to 15 minutes. When most of the moisture is gone, add onion and bell pepper. In a small bowl, mix together the flour and Tex-Mex Spice. When onion is translucent, add flour mixture to the pot. With a heavy spoon or spatula, toss meat mixture and scrape the bottom of the skillet until the flour browns.

Add water and bring to a simmer. When it simmers, cover and lower heat. Cook and simmer slowly until meat is tender, between 1¹/₂ and 2 hours. Check occasionally and scrape bottom of pan to prevent burning. Skim off fat, if needed.

Before adding tomato sauce, adjust gravy thickness to your liking by adding more water if necessary. Simmer on medium heat for 2 to 3 minutes. Add tomato sauce and stir. Season with pepper. Let it simmer for a few more minutes. Serve or hold in a warm oven. (If you used fresh tomatoes, let guisada sit for 3 to 5 minutes after turning off the heat.) Now it is ready to serve.

You can make up to two batches in a 4-quart skillet or pot, but reduce the water by 1 cup. Doubling the recipe only requires 3 cups of water.

MAKES 4 TO 6 SERVINGS

3 tablespoons vegetable oil

3 to 3¼ pounds round steak, cut into 1-inch cubes

1 cup coarsely chopped onion

1 cup coarsely chopped bell pepper

3 tablespoons flour

2 tablespoons plus 1 teaspoon Tex-Mex Spice (recipe on page 41)

2 cups water

4 ounces tomato sauce *or* 1 cup diced fresh tomatoes

Black pepper to taste

POLLO GUISADA

3 tablespoons vegetable oil

3 to 3¼ pounds boneless skinless chicken breasts, diced *or* sliced

1 cup coarsely chopped onion

1 cup coarsely chopped bell pepper

3 tablespoons flour

2 tablespoons plus 1 teaspoon Tex-Mex Spice (recipe on page 41)

2 cups water

4 ounces tomato sauce *or* 1 cup diced fresh tomatoes

Black pepper to taste

In a 4-quart heavy skillet or pot, add oil and bring to medium heat. When oil is hot, add chicken and sauté for 10 to 15 minutes. When most of the moisture is gone, add onion and bell pepper. In a small bowl, mix together the flour and Tex-Mex Spice. When onion is translucent, add flour mixture to the pot. With a heavy spoon or spatula, toss chicken mixture and scrape the bottom of the skillet until the flour browns.

Add water and bring to a simmer. When it simmers, cover and lower heat. Cook and simmer slowly until chicken is tender, between 1 and 1½ hours. Check occasionally and scrape bottom of pan to prevent burning. Skim off fat, if needed.

Before adding tomato sauce, adjust gravy thickness to your liking by adding more water if necessary. Simmer on medium heat for 2 to 3 minutes. Add tomato sauce and stir. Season with pepper. Let it simmer for a few more minutes. Serve or hold in a warm oven. (If you used fresh tomatoes, let guisada sit for 3 to 5 minutes after turning off the heat.) Now it is ready to serve.

You can make up to two batches in a 4-quart skillet or pot, but reduce the water by 1 cup. Doubling the recipe only requires 3 cups of water.

Variations: Boneless skinless chicken thighs work well for dark meat lovers; leave the chicken in large pieces. Gizzards work for country folks.

A guisada can also be made with pork. If you use pork chops or boneless pork loin, cut into 1-inch cubes. If using boneless country ribs or bone-in ribs, cut in half or quarters.

MAKES 4 TO 6 SERVINGS

EARLY TEXAS TURKEY CHILI INDIAN-STYLE

You will impress your guests more if you can use wild turkey instead of store-bought ... wild turkey has more flavor. Ground pork also works well.

1 pound ground turkey

1½ tablespoons cooking oil

1½ tablespoons cornstarch

1 tablespoon chili powder

1 large clove garlic, sliced

2 teaspoons dried leaf oregano

1 can (14½ ounces) whole *or* stewed tomatoes

1 cup fresh *or* frozen corn

1 cup finely chopped zucchini

¼ cup coarsely chopped sweet white onion

¼ cup coarsely chopped canned green chiles *or* bell pepper

2 whole chipotle peppers in adobo sauce *or* 1 tablespoon thinly sliced hot peppers

1 cup chicken broth

Using a cast-iron or nonstick skillet or pot, sauté the turkey in oil for 2½ to 3 minutes. Add the cornstarch, chili powder, garlic and oregano; sauté for 2 to 3 minutes. Add vegetables, peppers and broth, then simmer for approximately 5 to 10 minutes. Adjust seasoning to taste and serve immediately.

MAKES 4 SERVINGS

"I've been working on a new technique for soup. I cook the meat until it's perfect, then I take it out of the pot. I cook the vegetables until they're perfect, then put the meat back in. Everything is cooked perfectly that way."

PICADILLO

Here is my version of ground beef stew.

1 pound ground beef
½ cup chopped onion
½ cup chopped celery
½ cup chopped bell pepper
2 tablespoons Tex-Mex Spice (recipe on page 41)
2 tablespoons flour
1 can (14½ ounces) whole tomatoes, chopped
1 can (8 ounces) tomato sauce
1 cup water
¼ pound potatoes, peeled and thinly sliced (about 2½ cups)
2 cups fresh *or* frozen corn
Black pepper to taste

In a cold skillet or pot, combine the meat, onion, celery, bell pepper, Tex-Mex Spice and flour. On medium, heat to a simmer. Start stirring when you smell spice. When meat is no longer pink and vegetables are cooked, add tomatoes, tomato sauce and water. Bring to a simmer.

Stir in potatoes and corn. Cover and simmer on medium-low until potatoes are cooked, stirring occasionally. Season with black pepper.

MAKES 4 TO 6 SERVINGS

BLACK BEAN AND PORK STEW

3 cups dried black beans

4 cups water

2¼ pounds thin pork chops

3 tablespoons olive oil

2 large bell peppers, coarsely
chopped

1 large white onion, coarsely
chopped

2 jalapeños, seeded and chopped

3 cloves garlic, crushed

½ cup chili powder

1 tablespoon ground cumin

1 teaspoon salt

½ teaspoon black pepper

1 can (28 ounces) crushed tomatoes

1 cup (4 ounces) shredded sharp
cheddar cheese

¾ cup sour cream

Sourdough bread

Place the beans in a large saucepan and cover with cold water. Soak for 12 hours or overnight. Drain and rinse. Add 4 cups water to the beans. Bring to a boil and then reduce the heat. Cover tightly and simmer for 1 to 1½ hours or until beans are tender.

Trim the bone and excess fat away from the pork chops, and cut into ½-inch cubes. Heat olive oil in a Dutch oven over medium heat. Add the bell peppers, onion, jalapeños and garlic. Cook for 10 minutes or until vegetables are tender, stirring frequently. Add pork and cook for 6 minutes or until meat is no longer pink, stirring frequently.

Reduce heat to low and stir in the chili powder, cumin, salt and pepper. Continue to stir for 1 minute, then stir in the beans and tomatoes. Cover and simmer for 1 hour and 20 minutes. Add more water if needed. Transfer to soup bowls. Serve with cheese, sour cream and sourdough bread.

Variation: You can save time by making this stew with canned black beans instead of dried beans. Go ahead and skip the first few steps of the recipe (the first paragraph). Drain and rinse the canned beans and add at the same point of the recipe, with the tomatoes.

MAKES 6 SERVINGS

NEW MEXICO PORK POSOLE

This stew can be knocked off in 15 minutes if you really put your mind to it.

1 tablespoon oil *or* bacon drippings
1 pound ground pork
¼ cup coarsely chopped white onion
¼ cup coarsely chopped green chiles
2 cloves garlic, sliced
1 tablespoon chili powder
1 tablespoon cornstarch
1½ teaspoons dried leaf oregano
½ teaspoon ground cumin
½ teaspoon salt
½ teaspoon black pepper
1 can (14½ ounces) whole tomatoes, chopped
1 can (14 ounces) white hominy
1 cup chicken broth
2 whole chipotle peppers in adobo sauce

Heat oil in a large skillet (black cast-iron if you have it) to medium heat; sauté the pork for 2¹/₂ to 3 minutes. Add the onion, chiles, garlic, chili powder, cornstarch, oregano, cumin, salt and pepper. Sauté for 2 to 3 minutes.

Add the remaining ingredients and cook on medium heat for about 3 to 5 minutes. Then reduce heat and let simmer for 4 to 5 minutes. Adjust salt and pepper to taste, and serve immediately.

Variation: Ground turkey can be used instead of pork.

MAKES 4 TO 6 SERVINGS

CREAMY SHRIMP STEW

At a glance, this recipe looks like a major pain in the "ol' bee-hind," but it's not. Trust me, the little extra work is well worth the trouble.

1 pound medium shrimp with shells

4 tablespoons butter, *divided*

1 cup chicken broth

1 dry chipotle pepper

1 tablespoon flour

½ teaspoon salt

¼ teaspoon white pepper

¼ cup coarsely chopped white onion

2 tablespoons finely chopped celery

1 clove garlic, finely chopped

2 cups milk

½ cup half-and-half cream

2 tablespoons chopped cilantro for garnish

Peel the shrimp; set the shrimp aside. Place the shrimp shells in a small skillet or saucepan. Add 2 tablespoons of butter. Sauté on medium heat for 3 to 4 minutes. Add the chicken broth and chipotle pepper; simmer on low for 5 to 8 minutes.

While the shells are simmering, place the remaining 2 tablespoons of butter in a separate skillet. Add the flour, salt, pepper, onion, celery and garlic. Cook on low for 2 to 3 minutes, being careful not to brown the flour. Add the shrimp and cook 2 to 3 minutes more, frequently stirring and turning the shrimp.

To the shells and chipotle pepper, add the milk and cream. Warm to just under a simmer. Strain the shell mixture into the skillet with the shrimp (leaving the shells and pepper behind) and cook an additional 2 to 3 minutes on low heat. Serve in warm bowls, garnishing with the chopped cilantro.

MAKES 4 TO 6 SERVINGS

A MEXTEX FEATURE

SKILLET FAJITAS

Fajitas are a party food. They are meant to be fun and easy for those involved, so let me make it easy for you! The main ingredients are meat, chicken, shrimp or veggies, hot sauce and tortillas. (Figure ½ pound of meat and at least two tortillas per person.) Preferred garnishes are pico, guacamole, chile con queso, sour cream and shredded cheddar cheese.

Good sides are MexTex Rice (page 148), Refried Beans (page 145) or Charro Beans (page 142).

First, make sure your hot sauce, side dishes and desired garnishes are ready before you start cooking the meat. Then cut the beef or chicken into thin strips, or if using shrimp, shell and devein. Season with Texas Sprinkle.

In a 10- or 12-inch skillet, heat 3 tablespoons of oil to medium-high. Turn heat down to medium and cook meat 1 pound at a time: For beef, cook for 1 minute first, then add onions and peppers and cook 2 to 3 minutes longer. For chicken and shrimp, put down at the same time as the onions and peppers, and sauté for about 3 to 4 minutes.

Once meat is cooked, drizzle Black Magic over skillet and toss for 15 to 20 seconds. Place on a family-style platter and serve immediately with tortillas, hot sauce, garnishes and sides.

For Veggie Fajitas: Use a combination of corn, chopped broccoli, and sliced onions, bell peppers, mushrooms, zucchini and yellow squash. Allow 1 cup of veggies per serving.

Cook 2 cups of veggies at a time: Use 4 teaspoons Texas Sprinkle and 3 tablespoons oil. Sauté for 3 to 4 minutes on medium-high. When veggies are cooked, drizzle with Black Magic and toss for 15 to 20 seconds. I like to serve veggie fajitas on corn tortillas.

MAKES 4 SERVINGS

2 pounds beef sirloin *or* tenderloin, boneless skinless chicken breasts *or* thighs, *or* 16–20 count shrimp

8 teaspoons Texas Sprinkle (recipe on page 42)

6 tablespoons cooking oil, *divided*

2 cups sliced onions

2 cups sliced bell peppers

Black Magic Finishing Sauce (recipe on page 43)

8 to 12 flour *or* corn tortillas, warmed

MESQUITE-GRILLED CABRITO

Cabrito (baby goat) should be crispy on the outside and tender on the inside. It can be served cubed or shredded. This simple barbecuing technique also works wonders with ribs and chicken. Half the goat's weight is bone, so don't be misled by seemingly gigantic servings.

2 gallons water
3 tablespoons salt, *divided*
1 cup distilled white vinegar
6 to 8 pounds baby goat on the bone
2 tablespoons lard
2 cups warm water

Pour 2 gallons of water into a large tub; add the vinegar and 2 tablespoons of salt. Place the goat in the tub and wash it thoroughly.

While it's soaking, build a large mesquite wood fire in a barrel barbecue pit. The grate's cooking surface should be at least 24 by 36 inches. Burn the wood down to white coals, and make a 2- to 3-inch bed of coals under the grate by shoveling in the necessary amount of coals.

For the basting mixture, place the lard and remaining salt in a bowl. Add warm water and let stand until the lard and salt are dissolved.

Remove the meat from the tub. You can leave it whole or cut it into pieces. Place meat on the grate, roughly 20 to 24 inches above the coals. Roast the goat for 2 to 3 hours, turning it frequently and applying the basting mixture until goat is golden brown on all sides.

MAKES 4 TO 6 SERVINGS

Matt's dog, "Star," guards the patio pit out back, hoping for some scraps.

COWBOY STEAK TAMPIQUENO

Rib eye is my choice of steak for this recipe.

1 cup Ranchero Sauce (recipe on page 52)
4 steaks of your choice (6 to 8 ounces *each*)
Texas Sprinkle (recipe on page 42)
¼ cup flour
¼ cup olive oil
½ recipe Virgin Pico (page 153)
¼ cup shredded Monterey Jack *or* American cheese

Prepare sauce and keep warm. Season steaks with Texas Sprinkle, following the directions on page 42. Dust lightly with flour (about 1 tablespoon flour per steak). Heat the oil in a skillet and cook steaks to order. Place on a serving platter and keep warm.

Keep drippings in the skillet; stir in pico and ½ teaspoon Texas Sprinkle. Sauté for about 30 seconds to 1 minute. Spoon evenly over steaks. Pour ¼ cup warm sauce over each steak. Garnish each with 1 tablespoon cheese and serve immediately.

Variation: If you don't want to use Ranchero Sauce, add an additional cup of fresh tomatoes to the pico recipe.

MAKES 4 SERVINGS

CHICKEN MOLE GONE SIMPLE

This was a Sunday special once or twice a month when I was a child. We had it with tortillas, Spanish rice and beans.

4 cups water

2 pounds bone-in chicken breast halves

¼ cup coarsely chopped white onion

¼ cup coarsely chopped celery

¼ cup chopped green bell pepper

Pinch of salt

2 tablespoons oil of your choice

2 tablespoons flour

2 tablespoons chili powder

2 tablespoons creamy peanut butter

1 tablespoon roasted sesame seeds

1 teaspoon granulated garlic

1 teaspoon paprika

1 teaspoon ground cumin

1 teaspoon salt

½ teaspoon sugar

In a large saucepan, place the water, chicken, onion, celery, bell pepper and a pinch of salt. Bring to a boil, then reduce heat to low. Cover and simmer for 20 to 30 minutes or until the chicken is tender. Remove chicken from the broth and let it cool. Reserve the broth and vegetables. Skin, bone and shred the chicken.

In a large skillet, heat the oil over medium heat. Mix the flour into the oil to form a paste; in a few minutes, it will turn light brown. Stir constantly to avoid scorching.

Add the chili powder, peanut butter, sesame seeds, garlic, paprika, cumin, salt and sugar. Mix in the reserved broth and simmer for 5 minutes. Add the cooked chicken and simmer for 5 more minutes. Place in a large serving bowl and serve family style.

MAKES 4 TO 6 SERVINGS

WINO QUAIL

In a Dutch oven or other large pot, melt the butter over moderate heat. Dust the quail with flour, salt and pepper, then place in the pot. Add the onions, mushrooms, garlic and thyme. Toss and scrape the birds along with the other ingredients in the pot for 3 to 4 minutes, cooking until onions are translucent.

Add the broth and wine. Cook ever so gently with the lid on for 1 to 1¹/₂ hours, watching the broth so it does not get dry. Add water as needed and occasionally scrape the bottom of the pot. If the sauce is too thick, you may also add water until you reach the desired consistency.

When the birds are tender, add cream and gently simmer for 3 to 4 minutes. Season with salt and pepper to taste. Garnish with chives or parsley. Serve over rice.

4 tablespoons butter
6 whole quail or 8 quail breasts
3 tablespoons flour
¾ teaspoon salt
½ teaspoon white pepper
2 cups coarsely chopped onions
2 cups coarsely chopped mushrooms
3 cloves garlic, thinly sliced
⅛ teaspoon thyme leaves
1 cup chicken broth
1 cup dry white wine
1 cup half-and-half or heavy cream
Chopped chives or parsley for garnish

MAKES 4 TO 6 SERVINGS

A MEXTEX FEATURE

CHILES RELLENOS

Prepare meat and sauce; set aside. Preheat oven to 350°. Rinse the chile peppers and pat dry, making sure they are completely dry. Fill a skillet with ¼ to 1 inch of oil; heat to 375°. Roll each pepper around in the hot oil for 1 to 1½ minutes, causing them to blister. Remove the peppers and wrap in a damp cloth; let sit for 5 to 10 minutes. Then remove the skin, split each pepper, remove the seeds and all of the membranes.

In a bowl, mix the flour, salt and black pepper. Dust the peppers in the flour mixture. Roll them in buttermilk and dust again in flour mixture. Fry the peppers in hot oil until batter is golden brown.

Arrange fried peppers in a baking dish. Divide the meat evenly over the peppers. Top with sauce and sprinkle with cheese. Bake for 4 to 5 minutes or until the cheese starts to melt. While the dish is still in the oven, sprinkle raisins and pecans evenly over the rellenos. Continue baking for 1 to 2 minutes or until cheese starts to bubble. Garnish with sour cream and serve immediately.

Variation: You can use the meat and sauce of your choice. See other options in Matt's Mains and Spices & Sauces.

MAKES 6 SERVINGS

3 cups 20-Minute Taco Meat
   (recipe on page 95)
3 cups Ranchero Sauce
   (recipe on page 52)
6 large fresh Anaheim chiles
Oil for frying
2 cups flour
½ teaspoon salt
¼ teaspoon black pepper
2 cups buttermilk
2 cups (8 ounces) shredded cheddar
   cheese
¼ cup raisins
¼ cup chopped pecans

CHILES RELLENOS

The meats on pages 93, 95 and 96 can be used for chalupas, tostadas, enchiladas, tacos, quesadillas and many other recipes. When cooking with these meats, I usually make two to four servings more than needed. In general, 1 cup of meat yields the following quantities:

Four soft corn tacos

Three crispy tacos

Three flat tacos

Three soft flour tacos

Three enchiladas

Three tostada compuestas

Four meat and bean chalupas

SLOWPOKE BRISKET

8- to 10-pound beef brisket, untrimmed

Place unseasoned brisket fat side up in a roasting pan. Cover pan with foil and then add lid. Bake at 350° for 1 hour. Lower heat to 210° and bake 7 more hours.

When cooked, uncover and cool for 20 to 25 minutes. Place brisket on a large cutting board and separate meat from fat; discard fat. Coarsely chop meat into $\frac{1}{2}$-inch cubes. Meat can also be pulled or sliced. An 8-pound brisket will give you 16 to 20 cups of trimmed meat. Place in ziplock bags, 2 cups at a time, so meat does not dry out. Use immediately, save in refrigerator or freeze for later use.

ROUNDUP BEEF

4- to 5-pound beef eye round

Place unseasoned meat fat side up in a roasting pan. Cover pan with foil. Bake at 350° for 1 hour. Lower heat to 210° and bake 7 more hours.

Do not trim fat, unless you want extra-lean meat. Eye round is easier to work with than brisket, but it's not as sweet because of the lack of fat. Cut into $\frac{1}{2}$-inch cubes or shred. It yields about 2 cups per pound.

SHREDDED CHICKEN BREAST

You can use this shredded chicken for chalupas, enchiladas or tacos.

Rub chicken with oil and place on a baking sheet. Bake at 325° for 1½ hours. Internal meat temperature should be 180°. Turn off oven but wait 10 to 15 minutes before removing from oven. When cooled, remove skin, bone and shred with two forks.

Chicken breast, bone in and skin on with ribs
1 teaspoon olive oil per chicken breast

MAKES ABOUT 2 CUPS PER POUND

20-MINUTE TACO MEAT

You can use this taco meat for chalupas, enchiladas or tacos.

In a cold skillet, stir the bell pepper, celery, onion and Tex-Mex Spice. Spread uncooked meat on top. Turn to medium heat. When meat starts to simmer, stir and break up meat. Simmer on low for 20 minutes.

Variation: Lean pork or ground turkey also work well instead of beef. If using turkey, add 1 tablespoon olive oil with the veggies.

¼ cup finely chopped bell pepper
¼ cup chopped celery
½ cup chopped white onion
1 tablespoon plus 2 teaspoons Tex-Mex Spice (recipe on page 41)
1 pound lean ground beef

MAKES 3 CUPS

PULLED PORK LOIN

5-pound boneless pork loin

Place unseasoned pork loin fat side up in a roasting pan. Cover pan with foil and then add lid. Bake at 350° for 1 hour. Lower heat to 210° and bake 3 more hours.

When cooked, uncover and cool for 20 to 25 minutes. Do not trim fat, unless you want extra-lean meat. Pork loin is not marbled and needs a little fat. This meat can be pulled and lightly chopped before use. Loin will yield about 2 cups per pound. Place in ziplock bags, 2 cups at a time, so meat does not dry out. Use immediately, save in refrigerator or freeze for later use.

GETTING PULLED AND CHOPPED MEAT READY TO USE

For each cup of meat, you need:

½ teaspoon Texas Sprinkle (recipe on page 42)
1 teaspoon oil
1 tablespoon water

Mix meat and Texas Sprinkle in a bowl. In a cast-iron or nonstick skillet, heat oil to medium heat (it is ready when a drop of water sizzles in the skillet). Carefully add meat; turn heat to low. Cook and stir for 30 to 45 seconds. Add water and continue gently stirring. Cook for 1 minute. Turn heat off and it is ready to use.

Estella with her father, Gustavo Benavidez, near their Corpus Christi farmhouse.

★ 97

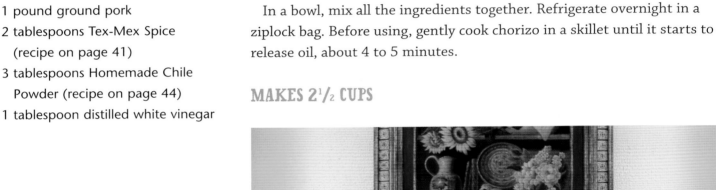

CHILE ANCHO CHORIZO

You can use this chorizo as a flavoring agent for beans, potatoes, eggs, migas and dips.

1 pound ground pork
2 tablespoons Tex-Mex Spice
  (recipe on page 41)
3 tablespoons Homemade Chile
  Powder (recipe on page 44)
1 tablespoon distilled white vinegar

In a bowl, mix all the ingredients together. Refrigerate overnight in a ziplock bag. Before using, gently cook chorizo in a skillet until it starts to release oil, about 4 to 5 minutes.

MAKES 2½ CUPS

HOME-STYLE RICE WITH SHRIMP

In a large deep skillet, sauté the rice in oil over low heat for 4 to 5 minutes or until the rice is wheat brown in color, stirring constantly. Add onion and garlic and sauté a few more seconds. Add bell pepper and tomato sauce; mix thoroughly.

Stir in the salt, shrimp and chicken broth. Bring to a boil. Turn heat down and simmer, covered, for 15 minutes. Remove from heat and let rest for 5 minutes. Very important: Never lift lid while dish is simmering or until after it has completed the 5-minute rest period. Fluff rice with a fork and serve.

Variation: If you like hot rice, substitute one peeled and chopped poblano pepper for the bell pepper.

2 cups uncooked long grain rice

2 tablespoons olive oil

½ cup finely chopped onion

3 cloves fresh garlic, mashed

½ cup chopped bell pepper

½ cup tomato sauce

1 teaspoon salt

1 pound uncooked shrimp, shelled, deveined and cut into ½-inch pieces

3½ cups chicken broth

MAKES 4 TO 6 SERVINGS

Cooking chuck-wagon style with (from left) Grady Spears, Tom Perini and Robert McGrath.

AUSTIN SHRIMP A LA MEXICANA

Make rice and sauce and keep warm. If shrimp is frozen, thaw, drain and pat dry. Season shrimp with Texas Sprinkle. In a 12-inch skillet or sauté pan, heat 2 tablespoons oil to medium heat. Add 1 pound of shrimp and sauté for 1 minute. Add 1 tablespoon of butter and cook 3 more minutes. Add Black Magic and stir for 5 to 10 seconds.

Place the rice in a 9-inch x 13-inch baking dish; spoon sautéed shrimp over rice and hold in a warm oven. Repeat process for remaining shrimp (cook 1 pound at a time with remaining oil and butter). Add to baking dish.

Pour 3 cups of Ranchero Sauce over shrimp; sprinkle cheese over the top. Pour remaining sauce over cheese. Bake at 375° for 8 to 10 minutes or until cheese is melted.

MAKES 8 TO 10 SERVINGS

1 recipe of MexTex Rice (page 148)

1 recipe of Ranchero Sauce (page 52)

3 pounds of 16–20 count fresh *or* frozen uncooked shrimp, shelled and deveined

Texas Sprinkle to taste (recipe on page 42)

6 tablespoons olive oil, *divided*

3 tablespoons butter, softened, *divided*

Black Magic Finishing Sauce to taste (recipe on page 43)

2 to 3 cups (8 to 12 ounces) shredded Monterey Jack *or* cheddar cheese

AUSTIN REDFISH A LA MEXICANA

4 redfish fillets (6 to 8 ounces *each*)

Texas Sprinkle to taste
(recipe on page 42)

4 tablespoons olive oil, *divided*

½ to 1 cup flour, *divided*

Black Magic Finishing Sauce to taste
(recipe on page 43)

4 tablespoons sour cream

1 cup Ranchero Sauce
(recipe on page 52)

1 to 1½ cups (4 to 6 ounces)
shredded Monterey Jack *or*
cheddar cheese

Season fish with Texas Sprinkle. In a skillet or sauté pan, heat 2 tablespoons oil to medium heat. Dust two of the fillets with some of the flour and place in the skillet; cook for 2 to 3 minutes per side or until golden brown and flaky. Add Black Magic and flip fillets once or twice.

Place fish in a baking dish and hold in a warm oven. Repeat process with the remaining fillets, flour and oil. Add to baking dish. Spread 1 tablespoon of sour cream over each fillet. Top with sauce, then sprinkle with cheese. Broil on middle rack for 2 to 3 minutes or until cheese is melted. Serve immediately.

Variations: Catfish can be substituted for redfish.

Instead of Ranchero Sauce, you can use a green sauce such as my Tomatillo Hot Sauce (page 50) or Green Simplicity Tomatillo Sauce (page 60).

CATFISH MARTINEZ

Many people think of catfish as "trashfish" because catfish found in rivers and streams are known to eat anything they can suck up. Farm-raised catfish are much different. They're probably the fish of the future. They are high in nutrition, low in fat and kitchen-friendly. I find them really easy to work with. I prefer fillets over the whole fish.

In a large skillet, preferably cast-iron, heat the oil to 375°. Apply Texas Sprinkle to both side of the fillets, then lightly dust both sides with flour. Place the dusted catfish in the hot oil; cook for 3 to 5 minutes on each side. They are ready when they are golden brown and soft enough to flake easily with a fork.

When the fillets are cooked to perfection, splash them with Black Magic while they're still in the skillet, then serve immediately. Serve with rice and grilled or sautéed vegetables of choice.

Variation: You can substitute the fish of your choice in this recipe, particularly trout, bass, crappie or perch.

MAKES 4 SERVINGS

3 tablespoons vegetable oil

2 teaspoons Texas Sprinkle (recipe on page 42)

1½ pounds farm-raised catfish fillets (fresh *or* frozen)

4 heaping tablespoons flour

4 tablespoons Black Magic Finishing Sauce (recipe on page 43)

ENCHILADAS & TACOS

In the late 1970s and early '80s, John Denver was giving a lot of concerts at the University of Texas. He'd heard we had some good cheese enchiladas at our restaurant, and that was one of his favorite things. He called and asked if we'd stay open late after a concert.

He had 60 to 80 people in his group, and he told 'em all what he'd heard about our cheese and onion enchiladas. So when I brought his out, he looked at them a little bit funny. I think he was used to the New Mexican chile enchiladas that had a deep-red chile sauce on top.

He looked at the person sitting across from him and shrugged, then he took a bite and said, "Man, these are good, but they're not very hot."

I told him, "We don't make them very hot because we have this hot sauce on the side, so you can make them as hot as you want."

So he poured a little bit on the side, took a little ol' bite and started shaking his head up and down. He asked for more chopped onions, so we brought him some, and he got himself a system going. With a corn tortilla in his left hand, he'd pour a little hot sauce on the side of his plate, eat a bite of enchilada, then kind of scoot it around with his tortilla. Every once in a while, he'd reach over to the onions and get a forkful and drop them on top.

He never said another word. He just finished cleaning his plate with the leftover corn tortilla. It was clean enough to put back in the rack.

"I just never knew, I just never knew," he said. "They told me the truth."

And every time he came in, it was the same thing. He wouldn't order anything else. He had everybody with him ordering our enchiladas, too—a few might ask for beef or no onions, but 80 percent of them would have those cheese and onion enchiladas.

Mr. Denver was an incredible gentleman, and I hope he's getting his cheese and onion enchiladas wherever he is now.

I was inducted into the Texas Restaurant Association Hall of Honor in 2000. My father, who was inducted in 1986, and I became the only father and son both to receive this honor.

CHEESE AND ONION ENCHILADAS

2 cups enchilada sauce of your choice*
1 cup vegetable oil
12 corn tortillas
3 cups (12 ounces) shredded cheese of your choice*
1 cup coarsely chopped onion

Get your ingredients together and warm your sauce. In a deep-fat fryer set at 350° or a 10-inch skillet on medium, heat the oil. Dip tortillas in oil for 4 to 5 seconds until limp. Place on paper towels to drain.

After all the tortillas have been dipped in oil and drained, dip them in warm enchilada sauce and stack on a cookie sheet or cutting board. Remove a tortilla from your stack, fill with 2 heaping tablespoons of cheese and about 1 tablespoon of onion. Roll up and place seam side down, side by side, in a casserole dish.

Evenly pour or ladle sauce over enchiladas. Sprinkle with the remaining cheese. Bake at 350° for 12 to 15 minutes. Remove from the oven and they're ready to serve.

* For sauce and cheese suggestions, see page 111.

MAKES 4 TO 6 SERVINGS

MEAT AND CHEESE ENCHILADAS

Around our house, we called these "payday enchiladas"—on payday we had meat and cheese enchiladas, and on the other days we had cheese and onion enchiladas … it was all about having money for meat. For "meatier" enchiladas, use 3 cups of meat and 2 cups of cheese.

2 cups enchilada sauce of your choice*
1 cup vegetable oil
12 corn tortillas
2 to 3 cups cooked meat of your choice, warmed*
2 to 3 cups (8 to 12 ounces) shredded cheese of your choice*

My grandfather Urbano Gaitan.

Get your ingredients together and warm your sauce. In a deep-fat fryer set at 350° or a 10-inch skillet on medium, heat the oil. Dip tortillas in oil for 4 to 5 seconds until limp. Place on paper towels to drain.

After all the tortillas have been dipped in oil and drained, dip them in warm enchilada sauce and stack on a cookie sheet or cutting board. Remove a tortilla from your stack, fill with 2 to 4 tablespoons of meat and 2 to 3 tablespoons of cheese. Roll up and place seam side down, side by side, in a casserole dish.

Evenly pour or ladle sauce over enchiladas. Sprinkle with any leftover meat and the remaining cheese. Bake at 350° for 20 minutes. Remove from the oven and they're ready to serve.

For Meat Only Enchiladas: Use 3 cups of meat and eliminate the cheese.

* For sauce, meat and cheese suggestions, see page 111.

MAKES 4 TO 6 SERVINGS

ENCHILADA SAUCE CHOICES

Beef Enchilada Sauce (recipe on page 56)
Creamy Enchilada Sauce (recipe on page 60)
Ranchero Sauce (recipe on page 52)
Sour Cream Sauce for Enchiladas (recipe on page 51)
Texas Original Enchilada Sauce (recipe on page 57)
Tomatillo Hot Sauce (recipe on page 50)
2006 Texas Enchilada Sauce (recipe on page 59)

When using the Ranchero or Tomatillo sauces, top with a dollop of sour cream. Use at least 1 cup per 12 enchiladas. If using Sour Cream Sauce, mix with 1 to 2 tablespoons of milk to soften for easier spreading on the enchiladas.

CHEESE CHOICES

American *or* White American
Cheddar *or* White Cheddar
Monterey Jack
Queso Fresco
Swiss

I prefer American cheese because of its smoothness and melting quality. When I use white cheddar, I like to blend it with one of the other cheeses. Queso fresco is a fresh white Mexican cheese that is slightly salty and has a crumbly texture.

MEAT CHOICES

Slowpoke Brisket (recipe on page 93)
Pulled Pork Loin (recipe on page 96)
Shredded Chicken Breast (recipe on page 95)
20-Minute Taco Meat (recipe on page 95)

PREFERRED MATCHES
RANCHERO SAUCE

- Cheese and Onion Enchiladas with any of the cheeses
- Meat and Cheese Enchiladas with brisket and a mix of cheddar and American
- Meat and Cheese Enchiladas with pork, chicken *or* taco meat and any of the cheeses
- Meat Only Enchiladas with brisket, pork, chicken *or* taco meat

BEEF ENCHILADA SAUCE

- Cheese and Onion Enchiladas with American *or* cheddar
- Meat and Cheese Enchiladas with taco meat and cheese
- Meat Only Enchiladas with taco meat

TEXAS ORIGINAL AND 2006 TEXAS SAUCE

- Meat and Cheese Enchiladas with chicken *or* taco meat and American *or* cheddar
- Meat Only Enchiladas with chicken *or* taco meat

TOMATILLO HOT SAUCE

- Cheese and Onion Enchiladas with Monterey Jack, queso fresco, Swiss *or* white American
- Meat and Cheese Enchiladas with pork, chicken *or* taco meat and any of the cheeses
- Meat Only Enchiladas with pork, chicken *or* taco meat

SOUR CREAM SAUCE

- Meat and Cheese Enchiladas with pork, chicken *or* taco meat and Monterey Jack, queso fresco, Swiss *or* white American
- Meat Only Enchiladas with pork, chicken *or* taco meat

★ 111

A taco can be as simple as a flour or corn tortilla and beans. We have soft flour or corn, crispy and grilled tacos plus an Austin favorite, the flat taco—it's a mini taco salad.

Get out your favorite hot sauce and a few side condiments. Don't go crazy ... keep it simple and fun. Set out the meat, tortillas, and any warm condiments such as queso or beans. I like to dress my shredded lettuce with a vinaigrette—try the Cilantro Vinaigrette on page 63.

SOFT FLOUR TACOS

6 cups cooked meat of your choice
18 to 24 flour tortillas (5-inch size)
Shredded lettuce
Chopped fresh tomatoes

Hold the meat in a warm oven. Warm tortillas on a hot skillet, one or two at a time. Place between a heavy folded cloth and keep covered. Never warm tortillas in the microwave—flour tortillas were not meant to be microwaved! They may be held in a warm oven if not used immediately. Serve meat and tortillas with lettuce and tomatoes and any other condiments you like.

Variation: In some circles, corn tortillas are favored, and they can be used in place of the flour tortillas.

MAKES 6 TO 8 SERVINGS

GRILLED TACOS

1½ cups olive *or* vegetable oil
24 corn tortillas
6 cups cooked meat of your choice, warmed
1 head lettuce, shredded
4 cups diced fresh tomatoes

Slightly warm oil in a skillet, just warm enough to touch. Dip a tortilla into the oil, then shake over the skillet to remove excess oil. Repeat. Pile all tortillas on a separate plate or pie pan, then put them aside.

Heat a large skillet to medium-high heat. Place one or two tortillas at a time in the skillet. Fry for 8 to 10 seconds per side until tortillas are very soft. Stack one tortilla on another on a plate.

Working on a flat work surface, spread ¼ cup of meat evenly on half of a tortilla and fold over. When all are filled, begin grilling three to four tacos at a time. Use medium to high heat in an oiled skillet until tacos are slightly toasted on each side. Place tacos on a large platter lined with paper towels and hold in a warm oven. When all are ready, serve immediately with lettuce and tomatoes, plus your favorite condiments and hot sauce on the side.

Easy Method: Not traditional, but it works! After sautéing and filling the tacos, place them close but not touching on a baking sheet (may require two baking sheets). Bake at 450° for 5 minutes on one side. Turn over and bake for 5 more minutes.

MAKES 8 TO 12 SERVINGS

CRISPY TACOS

Place taco shells in a preheated 250° oven. Immediately turn oven to low heat and hold until serving time—no longer than 20 to 30 minutes. Check to make sure the shells don't brown. Keep the meat warm in the oven at the same time.

You can also microwave the shells for 30 seconds; break one and taste for crispness. Heat 30 more seconds if needed or until crisp. Be careful not to burn.

Serve shells and meat with lettuce, tomatoes and any other condiments of your choice.

Note: Have some extra shells on hand in case of breakage. Sometimes store-bought shells might seem a little stale, but it is usually the result of moisture. Warming them will help.

18 to 24 crispy taco shells, chalupa shells *or* Flour Tortilla Toasties (recipe on page 119)
6 cups cooked meat of your choice
Shredded lettuce
Chopped fresh tomatoes

MAKES 6 TO 8 SERVINGS

With my father, Matt Sr., son Matt III and grandson Nicholas.

CHICKEN FLAUTAS

½ cup vegetable oil

24 corn tortillas

2 cups shredded cooked chicken

2 cups (8 ounces) shredded
American *or* Monterey Jack cheese

1 cup finely chopped white onion

½ cup finely chopped fresh tomato

In a heavy skillet, heat oil on medium. When it's hot, the oil should be just shy of smoking and it should bubble lightly when you dip a tortilla. With tongs, dip each tortilla in the hot oil, one at a time. First dip one side, then the other, for 2 or 3 seconds per side. Drain on paper towels, then stack on a plate.

Once all tortillas have been dipped and drained, make your filling by mixing the chicken, cheese, onion and tomato thoroughly in a bowl. Place about 2 teaspoons of filling on each tortilla, then roll the tortilla up enchilada-style, except roll it tighter than you would an enchilada. Place rolled flautas seam side down on a baking sheet or platter; flatten slightly to keep them from unrolling.

In the meantime, heat a griddle or cast-iron skillet to medium-high heat. Griddle should only be lightly greased, with no standing oil, since the flautas are already sufficiently oiled. Place flautas seam side down first on griddle. The melting cheese will seal the seam shut so the flautas won't unravel.

Depending on the size of your griddle or skillet, grill flautas in batches of three to six for 5 minutes on each side or until both sides are crispy. Place flautas on a baking sheet in a warm oven until all are grilled. Wipe griddle between batches to remove excess oil. Serve immediately with sour cream, guacamole and your favorite hot sauce.

Variations: You can substitute equal amounts of shredded cooked pork or roast beef for the chicken.

My green and red sauces go great with flautas. I prefer green with chicken or pork and red with beef.

MAKES 8 TO 12 SERVINGS

CHALUPAS & TOSTADAS

Corn and flour tortillas have come a long way since the days of the Aztecs and the introduction of wheat flour by the Spanish. Tortillas are the No. 1 ethnic bread in the United States. No bread is more versatile than the tortilla.

Corn tortillas are the foundation of Mexican foods. They can be enjoyed soft and hot off the grill, or made into chips, tostadas or chalupas. We make tacos of all kinds with tortillas. You can't make authentic enchiladas, chilaquiles or migas without them.

The aroma of the flour tortilla warming on a cast-iron skillet is enough to stimulate even the pickiest of eaters. It's multiplied tres-fold when a freshly rolled tortilla meets a hot skillet.

I tell my children that any man or woman who can make fresh homemade flour tortillas will never have trouble making friends.

The flour tortilla's simple ingredients are a Texas creation only found north of the Mexican border. It's not an easy task to find flour tortillas in Mexico, where tortillas are traditionally corn.

For convenience, tortillas can be bought premade, as can taco shells, tostadas and chips. Or you can make them at home using a store-bought product like the masa harina mix Quaker offers. Store-bought tortillas are getting better and better, too, but I stay away from low-cal, wheat or gimmick tortillas. I prefer the traditional tortilla.

I'll be making chalupas, tostadas, tacos and more, and I'll show you some of the tricks I've learned along the trail.

FLOUR TORTILLA TOASTIES

Use for dipping, nachos, chalupas or taco salads. Figure two tortillas per person.

Score whole tortillas with a sharp knife, making a shallow "X". Preheat oven to 275°. Place tortillas on baking sheets or directly on oven racks. (A standard oven rack will hold approximately 12 tortillas.) Bake for 25 to 30 minutes. Check at 25 minutes; if crispy, they are ready to use.

Matt at almost 3.

MEAT AND BEAN CHALUPAS

As a heavy appetizer, serve one chalupa per person. As a meal, serve two per person. This recipe can easily be doubled or tripled to serve a larger group. Chalupas are traditionally served with shredded lettuce, diced tomato, sliced pickled jalapeños, and chopped onion and avocado.

1 cup mashed pinto *or* black beans
4 chalupa shells
½ cup cooked meat of your choice
1 cup (4 ounces) shredded American, Monterey Jack *or* cheddar cheese

With a spoon or knife, spread ¼ cup of beans over each chalupa shell. Top each with 2 tablespoons of meat and ¼ cup of cheese. Place on a baking sheet. Bake for 4 to 4½ minutes at 450°, or broil for 2 minutes on the middle rack. Check your broiler to prevent burning. A little charring on the cheese is really good.

MAKES 2 TO 4 SERVINGS

★ 119

BEAN AND CHEESE CHALUPAS

The term "chalupa" comes from the Aztecs, who called a small boat used on lakes and rivers a chalupa. The Aztecs made a small masa "boat" and fried it in animal fat, then filled it with different goodies such as beans, meat, avocados and chiles. In early Texas, fried corn tortillas were used to make these Tex-Mex favorites.

Today fried flour tortillas are used for chalupas. I also use my own Flour Tortilla Toasties (recipe on page 119). From the chalupa come nachos, tostadas, compuestas, taco salad and Mexican pizza (see page 123).

As a heavy appetizer, serve one chalupa per person. As a meal, serve two per person. This recipe can easily be doubled or tripled to serve a larger group. Chalupas are traditionally served with shredded lettuce, diced tomato, sliced pickled jalapeños, and chopped onion and avocado.

1 cup mashed pinto *or* black beans
4 chalupa shells
1 cup (4 ounces) shredded American, Monterey Jack *or* cheddar cheese

With a spoon or knife, spread $1/4$ cup of beans over each chalupa shell. Top each with $1/4$ cup of cheese. Place on a baking sheet. Bake for 4 to $4^1/_2$ minutes at 450°, or broil for 2 minutes on the middle rack. Check your broiler to prevent burning. A little charring on the cheese is really good.

MAKES 2 TO 4 SERVINGS

TORTILLA PIZZA

Darrell Royal, the legendary University of Texas football coach, makes this pizza his "only" choice when dining at Matt's El Rancho in Austin.

Spread 3 tablespoons of beans over each tortilla; top with 2 tablespoons sauce. Sprinkle each with 2 tablespoons of Monterey Jack and 2 tablespoons of American cheese. Place on a baking sheet. Bake at 450° for 4 to 4½ minutes or broil for 2 minutes on the middle rack. Check your broiler to prevent burning.

¾ cup refried beans

4 fried *or* baked flour tortillas

½ cup Ranchero Sauce
(recipe on page 52)

½ cup *each* shredded Monterey Jack
and American cheese

MAKES 4 SERVINGS

MEAT AND BEAN TOSTADA COMPUESTAS

For tostada compuestas, my preferred meat choices are taco meat or shredded beef, chicken or pork. I like to use green sauce with chicken or pork, but red sauce works with everything.

They are traditionally served with shredded lettuce, diced tomato, sliced pickled jalapeños, sliced onion and avocado on the side. As a heavy appetizer, serve one tostada compuesta per person. As a meal, serve two per person.

1 cup mashed pinto *or* black beans
4 chalupa shells
½ cup cooked meat of your choice
½ cup red *or* green sauce
1 cup (4 ounces) shredded American, Monterey Jack *or* cheddar cheese
Sour cream, optional

With a spoon or knife, spread ¼ cup of beans over each chalupa shell. Top each with 2 tablespoons of meat, then spread 2 tablespoons of sauce over meat. Sprinkle each with ¼ cup of cheese. Top with a heaping teaspoonful of sour cream if you like. Place on a baking sheet. Bake for 4 to 4½ minutes at 450°, or broil for 2 minutes on the middle rack. Check your broiler to prevent burning. A little charring on the cheese is really good.

MAKES 2 TO 4 SERVINGS

BEAN AND CHEESE TOSTADA COMPUESTAS

1 cup mashed pinto *or* black beans
4 chalupa shells
½ cup red *or* green sauce
1 cup (4 ounces) shredded American, Monterey Jack *or* cheddar cheese
Sour cream, optional

With a spoon or knife, spread ¼ cup of beans over each chalupa shell. Top each with 2 tablespoons of sauce and ¼ cup of cheese. Top with a heaping teaspoonful of sour cream if you like. Place on a baking sheet. Bake for 4 to 4½ minutes at 450°, or broil for 2 minutes on the middle rack. Check your broiler to prevent burning. A little charring on the cheese is really good.

MAKES 2 TO 4 SERVINGS

GORDITAS ("LITTLE FAT ONES")

In a bowl, mix masa, mashed potatoes and baking powder together thoroughly with a pastry knife or wooden mixing spoon. Add cold water, 1 tablespoon at a time, mixing after each addition until the dough is no longer crumbly and can be shaped easily into little balls. *Don't add too much water.*

Divide dough and roll into 12 walnut-sized balls. Place on a plate or cookie sheet lined with waxed paper. Cover with another sheet of waxed paper to keep dough from drying out. Let them rest at least 10 minutes (longer if you have the time).

Add ¹/₂ inch of oil to a skillet; heat over medium heat. While oil is heating, flatten dough balls by hand. Work them with the tip of your fingers to form a 2-inch-wide circle. When oil is heated to just shy of smoking, drop dough circles into the hot oil. Depending on the size of your skillet, add two to three at a time. Cook for about 1 minute on each side or until golden brown. Drain on paper towels. Serve immediately with your choice of fillings.

Filling Suggestions: Crumbled fresh goat cheese, beans, guacamole and/or your favorite hot sauce. Shredded leftover roast beef, pork roast or chicken work well, too. Heat the meat up with a couple tablespoons of Ranchero Sauce first (recipe on page 52).

*Quaker brand instant masa harina is commonly found in grocery stores and works well in this recipe.

MAKES 1 DOZEN

1 cup masa harina (dry masa)*
½ cup mashed potatoes
1 teaspoon baking powder
¾ cup cold water
Vegetable oil for frying

On the Side

Main dishes might take center stage, but I think of sides as good ol'
comfort food ... a big pot of hearty pinto beans, a bowl of meatball
soup, a corn and squash casserole and my favorite rice are just a few of
the choices. You'll find pico de gallo here, too, to garnish that main dish
and make it complete.

My grandmother Maria Barbosa Gaitan.

I remember the first time I gave credence to comfort food. When I was about 8 years old, I was a little late for lunch—it was around 1:30, I guess. Coming out of the creek, I was a bit muddier than I should have been.

I saw my grandma coming around the side of the house. Her knees were real bad, so she was using an old mop handle for a walking stick. As she was calling out my name, she looked pretty angry. So I hid behind a post by our neighbor's house.

When she was out of sight for a minute, I slipped into a mud puddle in front of the neighbor's driveway. I slid in the mud and covered myself up. I lay there just as quiet as could be.

Grandma was about two feet away from me, still calling my name, but I dared not move, and I barely blinked. I did look up the road, though, and saw our neighbor, Mr. Torres, coming home. His car was getting closer and closer, and I guess Grandma was going to wait and talk to him, because she just stood there. He didn't see me in the puddle either.

I knew it was either move now or get squished by the car. So I jumped straight up in the air out of that mud hole. Grandma screamed, Mr. Torres screamed, and Grandma grabbed the creature that came out of the mud and started hittin' it with her stick ... just hittin' as hard as she could, 'til she realized it was me. Then she gave me a few more swats.

She drug me across the yard and into our backyard, made me take off my clothes and get in a No. 10 washtub. She filled it with cold water, got some Tide soap and a brush, then commenced to cleaning me real good. After she was done, she swatted me on the butt and told me to go in the house and get some clothes on.

I sat at the table for what was now a very late lunch. I had some vermicelli with ground meat and a little tomato sauce. Grandma also had a big ol' pot of beans, flour tortillas and a mild hot sauce. I remember how comforting that was, how soothing it was. I didn't at the time, but I think about it now—how something so simple can be so good. It didn't soothe the burning of my skin from the laundry detergent and the brush, but at least my belly was happy.

Whether you're 8, 38 or 68, it seems universal that people turn to Tex-Mex when they're in need of comfort food.

HOMEMADE STOCK

Use this recipe to make your own beef or chicken broth.
Turkey parts also work well instead of chicken.

2½ pounds beef neck bones *or* 2½ pounds chicken parts
10 cups water
1 rib celery, coarsely chopped
1 carrot, coarsely chopped
2 tablespoons black pepper
1 tablespoon salt
½ bay leaf *or* juice of 1 lemon

Wash beef bones or chicken parts well. Place in a stockpot. Add water, celery, carrot, black pepper and salt. If making beef stock, add the bay leaf. Bring to a simmer and cook for 3 hours. Skim top regularly and replenish with hot water to keep stock at the same level throughout the cooking process.

After 3 hours, strain into a large container. If making chicken stock, add lemon juice. If necessary, add water to make 8 cups of stock. Use immediately, or store in the refrigerator for 2 to 3 days, or freeze for later use. (After refrigerating, skim off the fat that has risen to the top before using.)

MAKES 2 QUARTS

COLD TOMATILLO CREAM SOUP

This soup also makes a great appetizer.

1 recipe of Green Simplicity
   Tomatillo Sauce (page 60)
1 cup half-and-half cream
1 avocado, finely chopped

Strain Tomatillo Sauce in a colander, mashing the veggies to get as much juice as possible. Cool slightly; discard pulp. Add cream and blend thoroughly. Refrigerate until chilled.

Before serving, stir chopped avocado into the soup. Add chicken broth or water if too thick. Serve in chilled bowls with tortilla chips or Flour Tortilla Toasties (recipe on page 119).

MAKES 6 TO 8 SERVINGS

TURKEY MEATBALL SOUP

In a bowl, mix the meatball ingredients. Form 6 to 8 meatballs and set aside. In a large pot, bring stock and water to a boil. If using fresh tomatoes, put tomatoes in boiling broth for 30 to 40 seconds. Remove tomatoes and place in an ice bath.

Turn heat down to a light simmer. Place meatballs, one at a time, on a large spoon and gently place in simmering broth. Put lid on pot and simmer for 30 minutes.

Peel tomatoes and coarsely chop. Skim broth and bring back to a light boil. Add chopped tomatoes, salt, pepper and veggies. Slowly simmer for 45 minutes to 1 hour.

Serve with corn or flour tortillas or cheese quesadillas. For condiments, try Bad Boy Hot Sauce (recipe on page 49) or thinly sliced hot peppers, lemon or lime wedges and chopped cilantro.

MAKES 4 TO 6 SERVINGS

Ground Turkey Meatballs:

1¼ pounds ground turkey

2 eggs, lightly beaten

½ cup finely chopped onion

½ cup finely chopped celery

½ cup bread crumbs

½ cup uncooked brown rice

1 teaspoon salt

½ teaspoon black pepper

Broth:

12 cups chicken stock (homemade *or* store-bought)

2 cups water

1 pound fresh tomatoes *or* 1 can (14½ ounces) whole peeled tomatoes

2 teaspoons salt

1 teaspoon black pepper

4 cups loosely packed chopped cabbage (½ small head of cabbage)

2 cups sliced carrots

2 cups green beans *or* peas

2 cups fresh *or* frozen corn

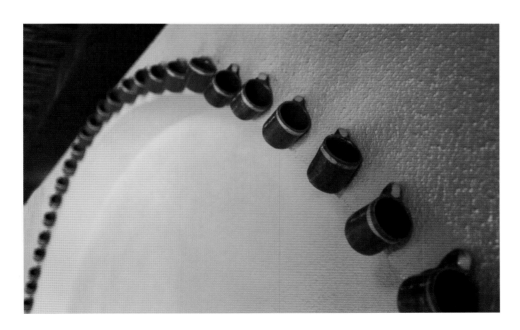

★ 133

Matt Martinez MexTex

AVOCADO CAESAR SALAD

One night in San Antonio, I was lucky enough to be hanging around Julia Child at a Southwestern cooking demonstration. She hated the fact that certain chefs were bastardizing a dish as classic as the Caesar salad.

"If you're going to make it different," Julia said, quite emphatically, "call it something else."

Oh, Julia, forgive me. It'll never happen again.

In a mixing bowl, combine the garlic, serrano chile, lemon or lime juice, olive oil, anchovy oil and Worcestershire sauce. Let the mixture sit for 5 to 10 minutes, allowing the flavors to blend.

Add the avocado to the mixture; use a fork or whisk to mix until smooth. Add the romaine and toss until the leaves are thoroughly coated. Add croutons, Parmesan cheese, salt and pepper, then toss again. Serve with anchovies on the side.

MAKES 4 TO 6 SERVINGS

1 clove garlic, finely chopped
1 small serrano chile, very finely chopped
3 tablespoons lemon *or* lime juice
1 tablespoon olive oil
1 tablespoon anchovy oil from can
¼ teaspoon Worcestershire sauce
1 ripe avocado, peeled and pit removed
6 to 7 cups hand-torn romaine
1 cup croutons
¼ cup grated Parmesan cheese
½ teaspoon salt
½ teaspoon white pepper
1 can (2 ounces) anchovies

My grandfather Delfino Martinez sold tamales and pralines on the steps of the Capitol before opening Austin's first Tex-Mex restaurant in 1925.

RUSTLER SALAD

I add fajita meat to my Rustler Salad to make it a main-dish salad. I like to serve it with my own Cilantro Vinaigrette, but you can use your favorite dressing instead.

Prepare fajita meat in advance and keep warm (or you can serve it cold if you like). Combine the iceberg and romaine; place a mound of lettuce in the center of each plate. Arrange tomato wedges around lettuce; top with avocado. Slightly overlap bell pepper rings neatly over each salad. Sprinkle with chopped cilantro and drizzle with vinaigrette. Top with fajita meat and serve.

MAKES 4 SERVINGS

1½ pounds beef fajita meat
1 head iceberg lettuce, shredded
½ bunch romaine, shredded
2 small tomatoes, each cut into 8 wedges
1 ripe avocado, peeled and cubed *or* sliced
1 small red bell pepper, cut into thin rings and seeded
1 bunch fresh cilantro, finely chopped
Cilantro Vinaigrette (recipe on page 63)

JALAPEÑO-LIME MARINATED SHRIMP

1 pound shrimp, shelled and deveined
1 cup chopped *or* julienned red bell pepper
1 cup coarsely chopped white onion
½ cup lime juice
¼ cup olive oil
¼ cup chopped fresh cilantro
2 cloves garlic, thinly sliced
1 jalapeño pepper, thinly sliced
1½ teaspoons salt
1 teaspoon sugar
¼ teaspoon crushed leafy oregano (Mexican oregano
   works best)
¼ teaspoon black pepper

Grill or broil the shrimp and let it cool.

In a bowl, mix the other ingredients and taste for seasoning. Add the shrimp and toss. Cover and refrigerate for 2 to 3 hours before serving.

MAKES 3 TO 4 SERVINGS

STUFFED AVOCADOS WITH SHRIMP

Grill or broil the shrimp and let it cool. Cut into $1/4$-inch cubes; place in a ziplock bag and cover with ice.

In a bowl, mix the celery, mayonnaise, sour cream, lemon juice, salt and pepper. Taste for seasoning. Add shrimp and blend.

Peel, pit and slice avocados in half. Place them on a bed of shredded lettuce; stuff the avocados with shrimp mixture. Garnish with onion, tomatoes and olives.

MAKES 4 SERVINGS

1 pound shrimp, shelled and
   deveined
1 cup thinly sliced celery
1 cup mayonnaise
¼ cup sour cream
Juice of 1 lemon
1½ teaspoons salt
¾ teaspoon pepper
2 ripe avocados
6 to 8 cups shredded lettuce
Sliced onion, chopped tomatoes and
   green olives for garnish

CHARRO BEANS

1 pound dried pinto *or* black beans

12 cups water, *divided*

6 ounces salt pork, sliced

2 cups chopped fresh tomatoes

1 cup chopped onion

4 to 6 whole fresh serranos *or* 2 to 3 jalapeños

2 cloves garlic, sliced

1 teaspoon salt

½ cup chopped fresh cilantro (loosely packed)

Sort and rinse beans. Place in a large pot; add 6 cups water. Soak overnight or for at least 6 hours in the refrigerator.

Drain beans. Add 6 cups fresh water and the salt pork. Bring to a boil; reduce heat and simmer for 1 hour. Then add tomatoes, onion, peppers, garlic and salt. Cook until tender, about 1½ to 2 hours. Add water occasionally to keep the beans soupy.

Adjust salt if needed. Add cilantro at serving time. Hold on low heat. Remove whole peppers and use as garnish, or break one or two and leave in the pot if you want spice.

For a special treat, add a whole zucchini squash with the tomatoes. You won't believe the smoothness and flavor. When serving, break off a little piece for each serving.

For Drunk Beans: Gradually add one Lone Star or lesser beer (at room temperature) while beans are cooking in place of some of the water.

MAKES 8 TO 10 SERVINGS

SPICY PARTY BEANS

These are great for serving a large group, but you can easily cut the recipe in half.

3 pounds dried pinto beans

3 quarts plus 2 cups water

2½ cups cooked chorizo

2 tablespoons oil *or* lard

3 cups coarsely chopped onions

2 cups coarsely chopped bell peppers

3 teaspoons salt

2 teaspoons black pepper

2 cans (14½ ounces *each*) whole tomatoes, chopped

½ cup sliced fresh jalapeños

Sort and rinse beans; place in a large pot. Add water and bring to a boil. Turn down heat and simmer gently. Cook for 2 hours, making sure to keep a half inch of water covering the beans.

While the beans are cooking, make the chorizo mix. In a skillet, gently sauté chorizo with oil or lard for 2 to 3 minutes. Add onions, bell peppers, salt and black pepper. Sauté 2 to 3 minutes. Add tomatoes and jalapeños and turn off heat.

After the beans have cooked for 2 hours, add chorizo mix. Cook slowly for 30 more minutes or until beans are soft. Adjust salt to taste. Leftover beans freeze well. Place 2 cups of beans in ziplock bags or freezer containers for handy later use.

MAKES 25 TO 30 SERVINGS

PLAIN OL' BEANS FOR REFRIED BEANS

Sort and rinse beans. Place in a large pot; add 6 cups water. Soak overnight or for at least 6 hours in the refrigerator.

Drain beans. Add 6 cups fresh water and the salt pork. Bring to a boil. Reduce heat; simmer for 1½ hours. Add salt. Cook until tender, about 1½ to 2 hours. Continue adding water to keep beans moist. Adjust salt. These can be eaten as is or refried.

To refry, heat lard slowly in a skillet. Carefully add beans; simmer and mash until smooth. Purists like a little more lard.

1 pound dried pinto
12 cups water, *divided*
6 ounces salt pork
  (optional but suggested)
1 teaspoon salt
1 tablespoon lard per 2 two cups of
  beans with juice

MATT'S HOG LARD

Use for sautéing and making refried beans, tortillas and gorditas.

In a Dutch oven or heavy pot, place water and salt pork with pork trimmings on top. Bring to a light simmer; cook for 25 to 30 minutes. Stir and continue to simmer for 1 more hour.

Lower the heat. Add bacon and cover pot with lid. Cook slowly for 2 to 3 hours. (If cooked in the oven, allow 4 hours at 200°.) Drain carefully through a sieve while still warm; use caution—make sure it is not too hot. Store in an airtight container after it has cooled.

1 cup water
12 ounces salt pork, sliced
3 pounds pork trimmings from your
  local butcher shop
4 strips bacon

BASIC BLACK BEANS

Black beans make a great side dish with any Tex-Mex entrée.

1 pound dried black beans
12 cups water, *divided*
6 ounces salt pork (optional but suggested)
1 teaspoon salt

Sort and rinse beans. Place in a large pot; add 6 cups water. Soak overnight or for at least 6 hours in the refrigerator.

Drain beans. Add 6 cups fresh water and the salt pork. Bring to a boil. Reduce heat; simmer for $1\frac{1}{2}$ hours. Add salt. Cook until tender, about $1\frac{1}{2}$ to 2 hours. Continue adding water to keep beans moist. Adjust salt.

TEX-MEX FIDEO

3 tablespoons vegetable oil *or* bacon drippings
1 package (5 ounces) vermicelli
2½ teaspoons Tex-Mex Spice (recipe on page 41)
½ cup coarsely chopped white onion
¼ cup coarsely chopped green bell pepper
¼ cup tomato sauce
2 cups water *or* chicken broth

In a large skillet, heat the oil or drippings over medium heat. Add the vermicelli; stir constantly for 3 to 4 minutes or until golden brown. Add the Tex-Mex Spice, onion and bell pepper; stir for 1 minute. Add tomato sauce and water or broth. Simmer on low heat for 7 to 8 minutes or until the vermicelli is tender to the bite but still firm. Serve immediately.

MAKES 4 TO 6 SERVINGS

MEXTEX RICE

4 cups chicken broth (homemade *or* low-sodium)

1 can (8 ounces) tomato sauce

3 tablespoons vegetable oil *or* lard

2 cups uncooked long grain rice

2 tablespoons Tex-Mex Spice (recipe on page 41)

½ cup chopped onion

¼ cup chopped bell pepper

¼ cup chopped celery

In one pot, heat chicken broth and tomato sauce until hot. Add oil or lard and rice to a 10-inch heavy pot or skillet (or larger). Sauté rice on medium heat until golden brown. Stir in Tex-Mex Spice; add veggies and stir for 1 minute.

Add broth mixture from the other pot and bring to a good simmer (but not boiling). Cover and cook for 15 minutes. Remove from heat and let rest for 5 minutes. Do not remove lid while cooking or resting.

Variation: Instead of the fresh veggies, you can use any 1-pound bag of frozen vegetables you prefer. Thaw first and then add to the rice right before adding broth and tomato sauce.

MAKES 6 TO 8 SERVINGS

MY FAVORITE WHITE RICE

If you'd like to make your own chicken broth for this dish, see my Homemade Stock recipe on page 131.

4 cups chicken broth (homemade *or* low-sodium)

½ teaspoon salt

1 teaspoon black pepper

1 medium carrot, cut into ¼-inch pieces

2 cups uncooked long grain rice

3 tablespoons butter

½ cup chopped onion

½ cup chopped celery

2 cups frozen peas

In one pot, bring broth, salt, pepper and chopped carrot to a light simmer. In another pan, sauté rice in butter. Once the rice is lightly browned, stir in the onion, celery and peas. Stir in broth mixture and bring to a good simmer. Cover and cook for 15 minutes. Remove from heat and let rest for 5 minutes. Do not remove lid while cooking or resting.

MAKES 6 TO 8 SERVINGS

"When I was growing up, the restaurant was closed on Tuesday, so our family would go out to eat. If we went to a restaurant we'd never eaten at before, my father would walk right into the kitchen. If it was clean, we'd stay. If it wasn't, we'd leave. He always asked for a lemon to be brought to the table, then he'd sit there and clean the silverware with the lemon and his napkin."

SUMMER TOMATO PICO

This pico is meant to celebrate summer tomatoes at their peak without overpowering them. Serve it with tacos, steaks, chicken, fish and fajitas. It's also an excellent garnish for guacamole.

2 tablespoons vegetable oil
1 tablespoon fresh lemon juice
1 small clove garlic, crushed and finely chopped
1 tablespoon finely chopped fresh jalapeños *or* serranos
¼ teaspoon salt
2 cups chopped fresh tomatoes (¼-inch cubes, peeled and seeded if desired)
1 tablespoon finely chopped white onion
1 tablespoon finely chopped fresh cilantro

In a bowl, mix oil and lemon juice with garlic, peppers and salt. Let sit for 10 to 15 minutes so salt can draw flavors from the peppers and garlic. Mix in the tomatoes, onion and cilantro. Serve immediately.

MAKES 4 TO 6 SERVINGS

SUMMER TOMATO PICO

PICO DE GALLO

Use this pico on the same dishes as the Summer Tomato Pico, but this version is more complex and traditional.

2 tablespoons olive *or* vegetable oil

1 tablespoon fresh lemon *or* lime juice

1 large clove garlic *or* ½ teaspoon crushed and finely chopped garlic

½ cup finely chopped fresh jalapeños *or* serranos, *divided*

2 cups chopped fresh tomatoes (¼-inch cubes, peeled and seeded if desired)

½ cup finely chopped sweet white onion

½ cup finely chopped fresh cilantro (loosely packed)

¼ teaspoon salt

In a bowl, mix oil, lemon or lime juice and garlic with only ¹/₄ cup of the peppers. Let sit for 10 to 15 minutes. Mix in the tomatoes, onion, cilantro and salt. Add remaining peppers gradually to suit your heat preference.

MAKES 4 TO 6 SERVINGS

VIRGIN PICO

This is a simplified version that works well as a topping or garnish for beans, guacamole, chalupas, enchiladas and tacos.

Mix all ingredients and serve immediately.

MAKES 4 SERVINGS

2 cups chopped fresh tomatoes ($1/4$-inch cubes, peeled and seeded if desired)

½ cup finely chopped sweet white onion

½ cup finely chopped fresh jalapeños *or* serranos

★ 153

MARTINEZ-FOSTER WITH PEACHES

This recipe serves 4 to 6 people, but you're probably going to wish you'd made more. I always do. I like to serve this alongside pork tenderloin or my Wino Quail (recipe on page 89), but it also makes a great dessert.

Melt butter in a skillet on low heat; stir in flour. Keep on low heat for the entire cooking process. Place the peaches cut side down in the buttery flour and cook for 3 to 4 minutes.

Flip the peach halves over; mix the brown sugar, cinnamon and cayenne together, then sprinkle over the peaches (mostly into the pit holes). Stir the brandy into the butter/flour mixture. Cook for 3 to 4 minutes, basting the peaches during the last minute.

Variation: You can use Jack Daniels instead of peach or apricot brandy.

3 tablespoons butter

1 tablespoon flour

3 fresh peaches, peeled and halved, pit removed

2 tablespoons brown sugar

¼ teaspoon cinnamon

⅛ teaspoon cayenne pepper (or a pinch)

1 ounce peach *or* apricot brandy

MAKES 4 TO 6 SERVINGS

STUFFED SUMMER ZUCCHINI

Fill a large pot with water and bring to a boil. Add whole zucchini and reduce heat; simmer until squash is al dente (about 10 minutes). Drain off water immediately and let squash cool. When cooled, cut each zucchini in half lengthwise; scoop out and save the pulp.

In a skillet, heat oil over medium heat. Add chicken, garlic and onion; heat for 30 seconds. Stir in the tomato, salt, black pepper and reserved zucchini pulp. Cook about 5 minutes more over medium heat, stirring as necessary to prevent scorching.

Place zucchini halves cut side up in a buttered baking dish. Spread chicken mixture evenly into zucchini halves; sprinkle with cheese. Bake at 350° for 10 minutes or until cheese is melted. Serve with tomatillo sauce if desired and garnish with a dollop of sour cream.

Variations: Instead of zucchini, substitute another summer squash such as yellow squash.

In place of chicken, use shredded or pulled beef or pork. Or use $^{1}/_{2}$ pound lean ground beef; brown the beef with oil before adding garlic and onion.

Instead of Monterey Jack, substitute longhorn cheddar cheese.

MAKES 6 SERVINGS

6 medium zucchini (about 1½ pounds)

1 teaspoon vegetable oil

1½ cups shredded *or* pulled chicken

1 clove fresh garlic, mashed

¼ cup chopped onion

¼ cup chopped tomato

½ teaspoon salt

¼ teaspoon black pepper

3 ounces shredded Monterey Jack cheese

Green Simplicity Tomatillo Sauce (recipe on page 60) *or* Tomatillo Hot Sauce (recipe on page 50), optional

1 cup (8 ounces) sour cream

BAKED SQUASH AND CORN

1 tablespoon butter
4 cups diced fresh zucchini
½ cup chopped onion
½ cup chopped green pepper
1 package (8 ounces) cream cheese,
  cubed
1 teaspoon salt
½ teaspoon black pepper
2½ cups cream-style corn

In a large skillet, heat butter; sauté zucchini, onion and green pepper over medium heat for 4 to 5 minutes. Turn off heat. Add cream cheese to the vegetables and mix well. Stir in salt and black pepper. Add corn and mix once more. Pour into a buttered 9-inch x 13-inch baking dish. Dot the top with bits of butter. Bake, uncovered, at 350° for 45 minutes.

Variation: You can use a combination of zucchini and yellow squash, or use any of the summer squashes. The important thing is to use the freshest squash you can find.

MAKES 6 SERVINGS

QUESO MAC

16 ounces large shell macaroni
2 tablespoons butter
3 cups chile con queso
Black pepper to taste

Cook the macaroni according to package instructions. Toss cooked macaroni with butter. Mix in chile con queso thoroughly. Add black pepper to taste and serve. Garnish with diced red ripe tomatoes or parsley.

MAKES 8 SERVINGS

ESTELLA'S ESPINACA AND PAPAS

Steam spinach for 3 minutes and drain; set aside. In a skillet, heat oil and butter; sauté onion over low heat for 3 to 4 minutes until onion is soft and just starting to brown around the edges. Stir often with a spatula to avoid scorching. Add tomato and mix well. Add potato slices and mix well. Add salt and pepper; mix well one more time.

In another 30 seconds, add spinach, but do not mix. Leave spinach on top and cook, uncovered, for 2 to 3 minutes over low heat. Flip spinach and ingredients beneath with spatula. Let rest another 30 seconds to allow flavors to blend. Serve immediately.

Variations: If fresh spinach is unavailable, use frozen spinach; thaw it first.

Substitute 1 tablespoon bacon fat for the oil; or omit the oil and use 2 tablespoons of butter.

Substitute green onion for the white onion.

1 pound fresh spinach, thoroughly
   washed and stems removed
1 tablespoon oil
1 tablespoon butter
½ cup chopped white onion
⅓ cup chopped fresh tomato
1 cup sliced cooked potatoes
   (round slices)
1 teaspoon salt
1 teaspoon black pepper

MAKES 4 SERVINGS

Celebrating my 30th wedding anniversary with Estella.

★ 159

PEPPERED FRESH SWEET CORN

6 ears fresh corn

4 tablespoons butter

½ cup diced white onion

½ cup diced bell pepper *or* pimientos

1 zucchini, sliced and quartered

1 teaspoon black pepper

Grate corn off the cob. Heat butter in a saucepan over medium heat; sauté onion and bell pepper until both are soft, but not browned (about 1 minute). Stir in corn, zucchini and black pepper. Cover and simmer over low heat for 10 to 12 minutes or until corn is tender. Serve.

Variations: If fresh corn is not available, use 6 cups of frozen corn instead.

Substitute poblano pepper for bell pepper. Roast the poblanos, remove skin and seeds, and cut into strips.

MAKES 4 TO 6 SERVINGS

MAMA MARTINEZ'S GREEN BEANS

3 strips bacon, finely diced

2 teaspoons flour

½ cup chopped white onion

1 clove garlic, mashed

½ cup chopped fresh tomato

½ cup water

½ teaspoon salt

¼ teaspoon black pepper

1 pound fresh green beans, cut into 1-inch pieces

Fry bacon until crisp; drain on paper towel and set aside. Reserve bacon fat. In a large saucepan, sauté flour, onion and garlic in bacon fat over medium heat for 1 minute, until onion is soft and translucent but not browned. Add tomato, water, salt and black pepper; mix well.

Add green beans and mix again. Cook for 3 minutes, uncovered, over medium heat. Cover and cook another 10 minutes over medium heat or until beans are tender, stirring occasionally. Garnish with reserved bacon bits.

Variations: Substitute ¹/₄ cup tomato sauce for the fresh tomato.

Substitute frozen cut green beans for the fresh beans.

For Vegetarian Beans: Substitute 2 tablespoons vegetable oil or butter for the bacon.

MAKES 4 SERVINGS

Eye-Openers

All your senses will be awake when you spice up a basic egg with peppers, beans, tortillas and chorizo. These recipes are so fast and easy, you can even make them on a morning when you're pressed for time. Once you've tried a plate of my migas or huevos rancheros, you'll never skip breakfast again.

MIGAS

12 eggs

½ cup chopped tomato

12 tortillas

4 tablespoons lard *or* bacon drippings (you can substitute butter *or* vegetable oil if you must)

¾ cup chopped onion

1 tablespoon plus 2 teaspoons Texas Sprinkle (recipe on page 42)

In a large bowl, whisk eggs and tomato; set aside. Tear the tortillas into 1- or 1½-inch pieces. In a cast-iron or nonstick skillet, heat lard on medium-high. Add tortilla pieces and sauté until crisp—be careful not to burn them. When crisp, lower heat and add onion; sauté for 1 minute.

Add Texas Sprinkle and mix well. Stir in eggs and cook until set. Serve on a warm platter with breakfast meats, refried beans and more tortillas. Garnish with hot sauce or pico.

MAKES 4 TO 6 SERVINGS

SUNDAY MIGAS

I like to serve this with sliced tomatoes and avocado, drizzled with fresh lime juice or vinaigrette.

If using bacon, coarsely chop and fry to taste (soft or crispy); drain on paper towels. Save drippings for frying tortillas if desired. Set meat aside.

In a bowl, mix the onion, tomato, bell pepper, garlic and Texas Sprinkle. Add eggs and mix thoroughly; set aside. Tear the tortillas into 1- or 1½-inch pieces. In a skillet, heat lard or bacon drippings over medium-high heat. Sauté tortilla pieces until crisp.

Add meat choice and toss for 30 seconds. Stir in veggie and egg mixture; cook and stir until set. Serve on a warm platter with refried beans and tortillas. Garnish with shredded cheese and hot sauce.

MAKES 6 TO 8 SERVINGS

Meat of choice: 6 strips bacon *or* 1 cup cooked chorizo *or* 1 cup cooked and crumbled sausage
1 cup chopped onion
½ cup chopped fresh tomato
½ cup chopped bell pepper
1 tablespoon chopped fresh garlic
2 tablespoons Texas Sprinkle (recipe on page 42)
12 eggs, beaten
12 corn tortillas
4 tablespoons lard *or* bacon drippings (or vegetable oil if you must)
2 cups (8 ounces) shredded American *or* cheddar cheese

Mom and Dad outside the original El Rancho location in Austin.

A MEXTEX FEATURE

HUEVOS RANCHEROS

Bacon, sausage, breakfast steak or pork chops make great sides. Cook your favorite meat before you start making the Huevos Rancheros. Refried beans, hash browns or fried potatoes are also good served with this dish.

Make the sauce and keep warm. Preheat four large plates in a warm oven. Tear the tortillas into 1- or 1¹/₂-inch pieces. In a skillet, heat oil; sauté tortilla pieces for 2 minutes on medium-high heat. Drain on paper towels. Place tortillas on warm plates, arranging them in a 4-inch circle.

Ladle warm sauce over tortillas (¹/₂ cup for each plate), spreading evenly. Add cheese in equal amounts over sauce. In a frying pan, cook eggs in butter over-easy or to your liking. Spoon over chips, sauce and cheese.

Variation: Instead of Ranchero Sauce, you can use my Tomatillo Hot Sauce (recipe on page 50) or your favorite hot sauce.

2 cups Ranchero Sauce
(recipe on page 52)
6 corn tortillas
3 tablespoons oil
½ cup shredded Monterey Jack *or*
American cheese
8 eggs
Butter for frying eggs

MAKES 4 SERVINGS

HUEVOS RANCHEROS

EASY BEANS AND EGGS FOR BURRITOS

12 eggs

Salt and pepper to taste

2 cups canned whole beans
(pinto *or* black) with liquid

2 tablespoons lard *or* bacon
drippings

12 tortillas, warmed

In a large bowl, whisk eggs with salt and pepper; set aside. In a skillet, warm the beans; simmer until most of the liquid is gone. Add lard or bacon drippings and simmer for 2 to 3 minutes. Crush half of the beans with a spoon. Stir in eggs and cook until set. Serve on a warm platter with warm tortillas. Garnish with hot sauce and shredded cheese.

MAKES 4 TO 6 SERVINGS

CHORIZO AND EGGS

12 eggs

2 teaspoons Texas Sprinkle
(recipe on page 42)

1 cup chopped tomatoes

2 tablespoons lard *or* vegetable oil

2 cups cooked chorizo

12 tortillas, warmed

In a large bowl, whisk eggs, Texas Sprinkle and tomatoes; set aside. Heat oil in a cast-iron or nonstick skillet. Sauté the chorizo for 2 to 3 minutes over medium heat. Stir in eggs and cook until set. Serve on a warm platter with warm tortillas and refried beans. Garnish with shredded cheese and hot sauce.

MAKES 4 TO 6 SERVINGS

PAPAS AND HUEVOS

In a large skillet, cook bacon until almost crisp. Place on paper towels. Heat the drippings (or drain and use oil) to medium-high. Add hash browns and cook until golden brown.

Lower heat to medium; add Texas Sprinkle, onion and bell pepper. Sauté for 1 to 2 minutes. Mix in cooked bacon. Add eggs and cook until set. Serve on a warm platter with warm tortillas. Garnish with shredded cheese and hot sauce.

MAKES 8 TO 12 SERVINGS

¾ pound bacon, cut into 1-inch squares
Bacon drippings *or* vegetable oil
1 pound frozen hash brown potatoes
3 tablespoons Texas Sprinkle
(recipe on page 42)
1 cup chopped onion
1 cup chopped bell pepper
12 eggs, beaten
Corn *or* flour tortillas (2 to 3 per person), warmed

Family Sweets

After a Tex-Mex meal, a cup of Mexican coffee or hot chocolate really hits the spot. Or how about a "martini" made with berries and brandy cream sauce? You can satisfy your sweet tooth with Texas pralines, the ever-popular sopaipillas drizzled with honey or my own tortilla-ice cream concoction that will leave your mouth watering.

BERRY MARTINI WITH BRANDY CREAM SAUCE

1 cup (8 ounces) heavy cream

2 tablespoons sugar

1 tablespoon brandy
   (I prefer Presidente brandy)

⅛ teaspoon vanilla

2 cups seasonal mixed berries

Fresh mint leaves for garnish

To prepare the sauce: Place the cream, sugar, brandy and vanilla in a blender; cover and pulsate on high until the cream gets body. Try not to blend stiff, but it's okay if you do!

To serve: Use ½ cup of berries and ¼ cup of cream sauce per glass. Spoon a layer of berries into each martini glass; add sauce and top with remaining berries. Garnish with mint.

Variation: Substitute your favorite fruit when it's in season, such as peaches, pears, melon or apricots.

MAKES 4 SERVINGS

ESTELLA'S FANCY FIGS

My wife created this recipe, which features figs and blue cheese with a brandy cream sauce topped with candied Texas pecans.

6 large fresh figs

2 ounces crumbled blue cheese

Fresh mint leaves for garnish

Candied Pecans:

2 tablespoons butter

½ cup pecan pieces

2 tablespoons sugar

½ teaspoon ground cinnamon

¼ teaspoon salt

Brandy Cream Sauce:

1 cup (8 ounces) heavy cream

2 tablespoons sugar

1 tablespoon brandy

   (I prefer Presidente brandy)

⅛ teaspoon vanilla

Quarter, slice or cube the figs (I prefer quartered). Set the figs aside at room temperature, and keep the blue cheese and mint in the fridge until serving time. Place dessert plates in the freezer (I like them really cold).

To prepare the pecans: Preheat oven to 325°. In a skillet on low to medium heat, melt butter; add pecans and toss until evenly coated. Place on a baking sheet and bake for 10–12 minutes. Mix the sugar, cinnamon and salt. Remove pecans from the oven and sprinkle with sugar mixture, tossing to coat evenly. Let cool. (If you're not ready to make the rest of the dessert right away, store the pecans in an airtight container or ziplock bag.)

To prepare the sauce: Place all ingredients in a blender; cover and pulsate on high until the cream gets body. Try not to blend stiff, but it's okay if you do!

To serve: Spread cream sauce on cold dessert plates (about 1 to 1½ tablespoons on each, distributed evenly). Place figs over sauce, then crumble blue cheese over the figs. Sprinkle each with a heaping teaspoonful of candied pecans. Garnish with mint and serve immediately.

MAKES 4 TO 6 SERVINGS

MAMA MARTINEZ'S SWEET POTATO CUSTARD

1 cup mashed cooked sweet potato

1½ cups milk

½ cup firmly packed brown sugar

½ teaspoon ground cinnamon

½ teaspoon salt

¼ teaspoon ground ginger

¼ teaspoon freshly grated orange zest

3 eggs, lightly beaten

Preheat oven to 350°. In a large bowl, combine all ingredients except eggs and stir thoroughly. Then add lightly beaten eggs and mix with a spoon until completely smooth.

Fill a roasting pan with $1^1/_2$ inches of hot water. Pour custard into individual cups or one 9-inch baking dish. Place in the roasting pan. Bake, uncovered, for 45 minutes (for individual cups) or 1 hour (for baking dish) or until a knife blade inserted in the center comes out clean.

Cool completely, then refrigerate for 2 to 3 hours before serving. Garnish with a dab of whipped cream and a sprinkle of pecan dust.

Variation: Substitute an equal amount of mashed cooked pumpkin for the sweet potato.

MAKES 6 SERVINGS

A MEXTEX FEATURE

EARLY TEXAS PECAN PRALINES

This is another of my mom's recipes. She also makes these candies with buttermilk (see page 180).

Mix sugar, milk and baking soda in a large heavy saucepan. Cook over medium heat, stirring constantly and scraping the bottom of the pan to prevent milk from scorching. After about 12 to 15 minutes, the mixture will start to thicken. (To test for doneness, drop a small amount of milk syrup into cold water. If it forms a ball in the water, the syrup has cooked sufficiently.)

Once syrup is ready, remove from the heat and add butter and vanilla; mix until creamy. Then stir in pecans so they are thoroughly coated. Quickly drop mixture by heaping tablespoonfuls onto a buttered baking sheet or piece of waxed paper. Let cool until solid.

When candies are cool, place in a covered container. They will keep 2 to 3 days at room temperature.

MAKES 2 DOZEN

2 cups sugar
¾ cup milk
½ teaspoon baking soda
1 tablespoon butter
1 ½ teaspoons vanilla
1 ½ cups pecan halves *or* pieces

EARLY TEXAS PECAN PRALINES

EARLY TEXAS BUTTERMILK PRALINES

1 cup buttermilk

1 teaspoon baking soda

2 cups sugar

2 tablespoons corn syrup

2 tablespoons butter

1 teaspoon vanilla

1 cup chopped pecans

Stir the buttermilk and baking soda in a large heavy saucepan. Cook over medium heat. Add sugar, corn syrup and butter, stirring constantly and scraping the bottom of the pan to prevent milk from scorching. Cook until mixture browns. (To test for doneness, drop a small amount of milk syrup into cold water. If it forms a ball in the water, the syrup has cooked sufficiently.)

Once syrup is ready, remove from the heat and add butter and vanilla; mix until creamy. Then stir in pecans so they are thoroughly coated. Quickly drop mixture by heaping tablespoonfuls onto a buttered baking sheet or piece of waxed paper. Let cool until solid.

When candies are cool, place in a covered container. They will keep 2 to 3 days at room temperature. They can also be frozen in ziplock bags for several weeks.

MAKES 2 DOZEN

MANGOS WITH WHIPPED CREAM

In a large glass dish, mix the mango pieces, oranges, sugar and lime juice. Chill for 1 to 2 hours. Serve in parfait glasses. Garnish with a healthy dollop of whipped cream and a sprinkling of pecan pieces.

Variation: Substitute ice cream for whipped cream.

MAKES 6 TO 8 SERVINGS

2 mangos, peeled and cubed

2 oranges, peeled, seeded and cut up (about 2 cups)

¼ cup sugar

1 tablespoon fresh lime juice

2 cups (16 ounces) heavy cream, whipped

1 cup pecan pieces

SOURDOUGH SOPAIPILLAS

Be prepared to make extra of these—most people will want more than one!

Vegetable oil for fying
1 can of 12 sourdough biscuits
    (quantities per can may vary, so
    you might need 2 cans)
¼ cup sugar
½ teaspoon ground cinnamon

Fill a skillet half full with oil and heat to 350°. On a floured board, flatten each biscuit as thin as possible. Carefully place the biscuits one at a time into the skillet. Fry for about 1 minute per side or until golden brown. Drain on paper towels. Mix the sugar and cinnamon together and sprinkle over sopaipillas. Serve hot with honey and butter.

MAKES 1 DOZEN

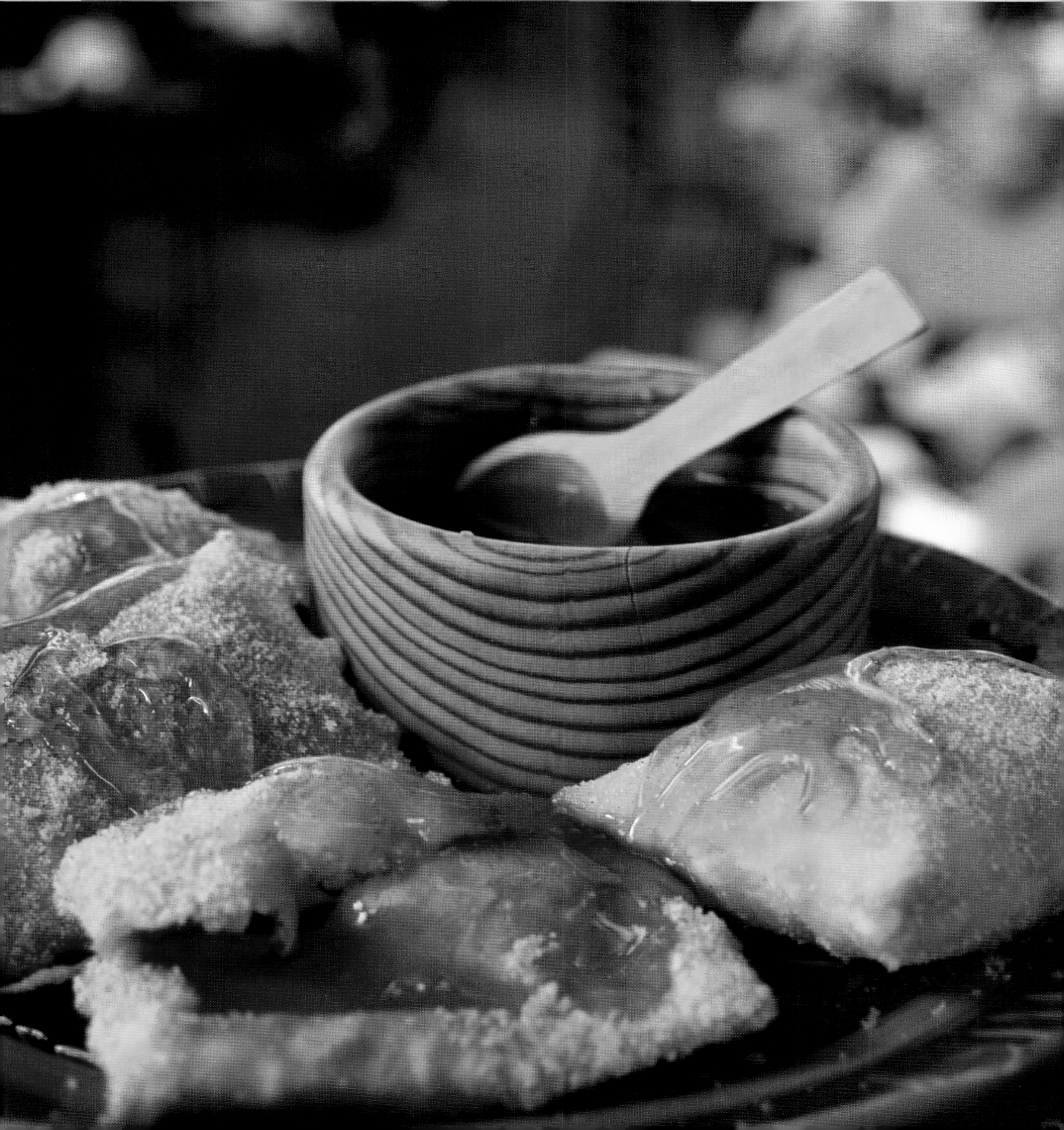

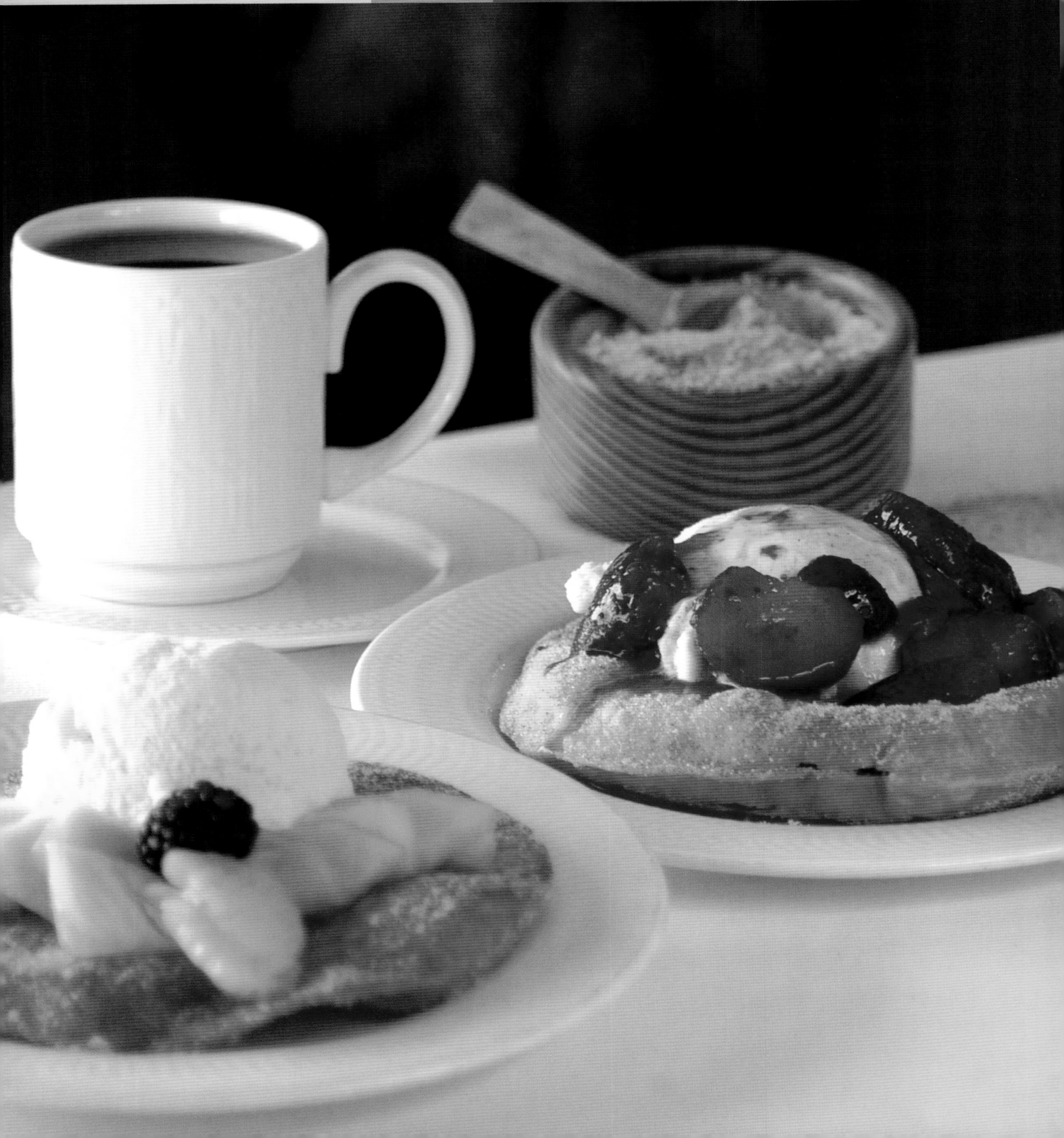

SWEET TOASTIES

Use any flavor of ice cream you like. Chocolate syrup and fresh berries make great toppings.

3 tablespoons sugar

1 teaspoon ground cinnamon

8 to 10 flour tortillas (6-inch size)

Butter for basting

1 scoop ice cream per tortilla

In a bowl, combine sugar and cinnamon; set aside. Preheat oven to 275°. Place a soda can or can of comparable size (a small tomato sauce can also works) just left of center on each tortilla and press down like you're using a cookie cutter (this will create a hole for the ice cream).

Baste both sides of tortillas with butter and sprinkle with cinnamon-sugar. Place on a baking sheet. Bake for 25 to 30 minutes. (Place an extra tortilla in the oven for testing … check at 25 minutes—if it's crispy, they're ready to use.) Place tortillas on dessert plates and drop a scoop of ice cream in the hole. Serve immediately.

Fried Method: Fill skillet a quarter full with vegetable or corn oil and heat to 350°. After cutting out the circle in the tortilla, fry in the oil until golden brown (about 1¹/₂ minutes per side). Drain on paper towels. Place fried tortillas on dessert plates; sprinkle with cinnamon-sugar and top with a scoop of ice cream. Serve immediately.

MAKES 8 TO 10 SERVINGS

MEXICAN COFFEE

¾ ounce brandy
¾ ounce Kahlua
Brewed coffee of your choice
Whipped cream

Mix brandy and Kahlua in a warm mug. Fill with coffee and top with a dollop of whipped cream.

MAKES 1 SERVING

DAMN HOT CHOCOLATE

1 cup Tia Maria Hot Chocolate Mix
1¼ ounces Hot Damn Cinnamon Schnapps
Whipped cream

Prepare the hot chocolate mix according to package directions. In a warm mug, mix hot chocolate with schnapps and top with whipped cream.

MAKES 1 SERVING

SWEET POTATO EGGNOG WITH DARK RUM

1 gallon eggnog of your choice

2 cups mashed cooked *or* canned sweet potatoes

1 tablespoon crumbled brown sugar

1 teaspoon cinnamon

½ teaspoon cayenne pepper

Your favorite dark rum (as much as you like)

Peppermint schnapps

1 cup powdered sugar

Place the eggnog in a mixing bowl. Thoroughly blend in the sweet potatoes, brown sugar, cinnamon and cayenne. Add the dark rum and stir.

Rim each glass with peppermint schnapps, then dip in the powdered sugar. Fill glasses with eggnog and serve.

MAKES 8 TO 10 SERVINGS

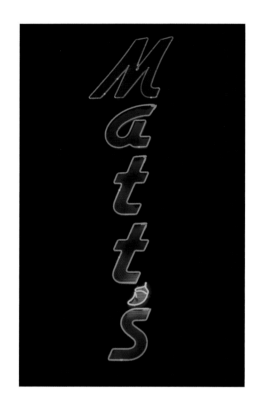

INDEX

ACKNOWLEDGMENTS

A big thanks to Rue Judd at Bright Sky Press for giving me the opportunity to do what I love—to cook, tell stories and teach other people my cooking techniques.

Thanks to her talented team: Designer Isabel Lasater Hernandez, for her creativity and great sense of design; Photographer Mark Davis, for truly capturing the beauty of my food and the ambience of our restaurants; and Editor Kristine Krueger, for making sense of my recipes and stories. I always knew my food tasted great and looked pretty, but this team really outdid themselves.

Thanks to Kim Hammond for keeping me on schedule and helping me keep my recipes simple and user-friendly. When you've been cooking your whole life, it's easy to make assumptions and skip steps here and there. Having her as a sounding board really helped keep me on track.

Most of all, I need to thank my family. Contributions from my mother, Janie Martinez; my wife, Estella; and my children, Matt III, Christine, Joaquin and Marco; really make this book even more special.

Aside from her recipe contributions, I have to give Estella a special thanks for all her patience and support … for allowing me to turn our kitchen into a late-night test kitchen and for cleaning up after me. Oh, and thanks to my dog, "Star," for eating all my mistakes—luckily, there weren't too many!